THE WEAK TWO BID IN BRIDGE

THE WEAK TWO BID IN BRIDGE

REVISED EDITION

HAROLD FELDHEIM

Foreword by Tannah Hirsch

C & T Bridge Supplies
3838 Catalina St
Los Alamitos, Ca. 90720

Artwork by Elizabeth Winston

To my wife Susan who typed the
book and to Al Roth who is the
Book.

TABLE OF CONTENTS

Forward   7

Introduction   9

Chapter 1: THE WEAK TWO BID   11

Chapter 2: RESPONSES and REBIDS   25

Chapter 3: THE STRONG TWO CLUB BID   45

Chapter 4: DEFENSE AGAINST THE WEAK 2   69

Chapter 5: CONVENTIONAL VARIANTS   99

Chapter 6: MORE ADVANCED CONCEPTS   119

Chapter 7: INTO THE NINETIES   127

FOREWORD

IN THE PAST DECADE, there have been tremendous advances in the theory of bidding, due largely to the spectacular successes of Italy's famed Blue Team in international competition, which has focused attention on their methods.

In Ecclesiastes, however, we are told: " ... there is no new thing under the sun." The Blue Club, most popular of the three systems used by the members of the Blue Team, is based on the Vanderbilt Club, invented by the father of Contract Bridge, the late Harold S. Vanderbilt, and almost as old as the game of contract itself. And part of the Vanderbilt arsenal was the weak two bid in the major suits.

Developed in the early 1930's, incorporated into the Vanderbilt Club system, and polished into its present form by Howard Schenken, the weak two bid has become the stock in trade of the vast majority of tournament players, yet it is very difficult to find a complete explanation of this convention and the theory behind it. With the exception of a chapter in Howard Schenken's "Big Club" most references to the weak two bid in bridge literature are brief and stress only the preemptive aspects of the bid -- completely overlooking one of the more valuable facets of the weapon -- its offensive potential. Properly used, the bid is most descriptive and allows close games to be reached that are difficult, if not impossible, to be bid in "standard" methods.

Next to Blackwood, the weak two bid is perhaps the most misused convention in bridge today, despite Howard Schenken's warning: "Dangerous if used improperly!" Even in international competition, the bid has had what can at best be described as limited success, not because of any weakness in the bid itself, but because its practitioners cannot resist the temptation to take liberties, and this usually courts disaster.

Here then for the first time is a complete book on the weak two bid. The methods advocated have been tried and tested at the highest levels of competition, and have proved successful. Follow the advice contained in these pages and your scores will improve.

But be warned: To use the weak two bid and achieve good results requires discipline. Exercise it.

TANNAH HIRSCH
Editor, A.C.B.L. Bulletin

Stamford, Conn.
June 1971

INTRODUCTION

A PROTOTYPE OF THE MODERN WEAK TWO BID was used as early as the early 1930's, but it was not until the mid-40's that Howard Schenken introduced the weak two bid in a form that is recognizable today. In the capable hands of Mr. Schenken, the weak two bid "wreaked havoc" among the great and near-great of the day. Quick to see its advantages, Alvin Roth adopted the weak two bid as a basic part of the new Roth-Stone structure of bidding. A short time later, Edgar Kaplan and Alfred Sheinwold incorporated the weak two bid in their now widely accepted but then revolutionary, Kaplan-Sheinwold bidding system. Why did this new method cause such a unanimous interest among the bridge pundits of the day? Simply, the weak two bid is a unique compromise between the "attacking" one bid and the "defensive" preemptive three bid. The weak two bid not only serves to effectively cut the lines of enemy bidding, but it also gives a phenomenally accurate picture of the hand, permitting partner to make judgments relating to the aggressive potentials of the combined strength. As an illustration, assume that you are in second seat with the following:

    ♠ J 9 3   ♡ A Q 9 8 5   ◊ K 8   ♣ K Q 8

This is a solid opening bid of one heart. Undisturbed, there should be no problem bidding this hand. Suddenly, your right hand opponent opens the bidding with two spades. You ascertain that he is showing a six card spade suit and between six and twelve points. Now you have to take some action on this hand and you realize that whatever you do may be wrong. If you bid your heart suit and your left hand opponent has a good hand with hearts, he will double you for a resounding penalty. If you pass, you may end up defending two spades, with a cold game available for your side. Partner's hand might be:

    ♠ 8 2   ♡ K 10 3 2   ◊ Q 9 7 4   ♣ A 4 3

in which case four hearts is cold -- or partner's hand might be:

    ♠ K 6 2   ♡ 7 2   ◊ A Q 9 7 2   ♣ 9 7 2

in which case the likelihood is that there is no good three level contract. Each hand contains nine high card points, and if you and your left hand opponent pass, with either hand partner will pass and end the auction. Notice that if there were no interference, you and partner could have determined with minimum difficulty whether or not the hands fit well. As it is, the opponent's two spade bid plunged you into the unknown. The particularly annoying feature is that if you make the correct "guess" there will be no great reward. You will simply achieve a normal result. If, on the other hand, you decide on the incorrect action, your results might range from inferior to catastrophically bad.

One of the questions that may come to mind is "What happens when the fates smile upon us and we are dealt a strong hand?" This question will be treated in full in a later chapter but for now suffice it to say that there will be no problem.

The weak two bid is a powerful weapon, and as with any powerful weapon, we must learn how to use and control it. The rewards will be not only a new and accurate bidding tool for our arsenal, but the pleasure of confounding those nasty opponents who always hold better cards than we do.

Chapter 1

THE WEAK TWO BID

1

THE WEAK TWO BID IS MADE IN diamonds, hearts or spades.*
As with any other conventional call, correct usage of the weak two
bid is governed by certain constraints. The rules and regulations
for the weak two bid are quite simple and quite logical:
   A.   The weak two bidder's suit should be six cards long.
   B.   The strength (high card points) of the hand should be between
        six and twelve points.
   C.   The weak two bidder's hand should, in most cases, not contain
        more than one control card (ace or king) outside the trump
        suit.
   D.   The hand should, ideally, not contain a void.
   E.   Preferably, the weak two bidder's hand should not contain an
        outside four card major.
Now let's take each of these five rules apart to see what makes
them tick.

A.   THE WEAK TWO BIDDER'S SUIT SHOULD BE SIX CARDS LONG.

   A seven card suit or even a superb five card suit may occasionally be suitable for a weak two bid, but by and large the weak two
bidder's suit should be six cards in length. In addition, the suit
must be of a playable quality. A good rule of thumb might be that
if partner holds a doubleton honor, the suit should produce at most
one loser. The minimum acceptable "texture" of the suit is depend-

---

*An opening bid of two clubs is reserved for strong hands. The methods of using
the artificial two club bid, together with the various responses and rebids are
discussed in Chapter III. For the moment, it is sufficient to realize that there
is no problem describing a strong two bid via the two club route, and this frees
the other three suits for our purposes.

ent on several factors such as the vulnerability and whether or not partner is a passed hand.* Examples of suits that can be opened as weak two bids are:

K Q 10 8 5 2
Q J 10 9 7 4
A K J 9 8 4
A Q J 9 7 4
K J 10 9 7 3

Examples of suits that should not be opened as weak two bids due to their poor quality are:

J 7 5 4 3 2
Q 9 5 4 3 2
K 8 6 5 4 3
A 9 8 7 5 4
J 10 8 5 3 2

B. THE HIGH CARD STRENGTH SHOULD BE BETWEEN SIX AND TWELVE POINTS.

Simple logic states that less than six points would tend to be too dangerous while more than twelve points is an opening one bid. Here, special attention should be paid to the vulnerability situation. When vulnerable, especially against non-vulnerable opponents, it is advisable not to open a weak two bid with less than nine high card points plus an acceptable suit. (See examples of biddable suits in Section A.) Not vulnerable, the weak two bidder should have not more than ten high card points, and the suit does not have to be quite as good as with a vulnerable weak two bid. Not vulnerable against vulnerable opponents, even greater liberties may be taken. After two passes against vulnerable opponents, it would be quite acceptable to open a weak two bid on a hand as weak as:

♠ Q 10 9 8 4 3   ♡ K 3 2   ◇ J 2   ♣ 9 7

since, with a passed partner, an opportunity to interfere with the opponents' bidding should not be missed.

---

*This concept of whether or not partner is a passed hand, i.e., the third and fourth seat weak two bid openings, will be discussed in greater detail toward the end of this chapter.

To summarize:

The approximate range for a vulnerable weak two bid is from nine to twelve high card points.

The approximate range for a non-vulnerable weak two bid is from six to ten high card points.

C. THE WEAK TWO BIDDER'S HAND SHOULD, IN MOST CASES, NOT CONTAIN MORE THAN ONE CONTROL CARD (ACE OR KING) OUTSIDE THE TRUMP SUIT.

Ideally, the weak two bid should contain one top honor card (ace or king) outside the trump suit, but not more than one top honor card since the hand would then be too strong for a weak two bid. As an example, a hand such as:

♠ K Q 10 4 3 2   ♡ A 4 3   ◊ K 3   ♣ 10 2

would be too strong for a weak two bid since, in addition to the twelve high card points, we should add one point for each doubleton and one point for the spade length, enough for an opening bid of one spade. Remove either the ace of hearts or the king of diamonds from the hand, and it is a perfect weak two bid at any vulnerability. With an eleven or twelve point hand, the decision whether to open the bidding at the one level or at the two level should be based on the control cards held in the side suits. As an example:

♠ K J 10 8 7 2   ♡ K J 3   ◊ 9 2   ♣ A 2

is a twelve point hand that should be opened one spade at any vulnerability. On the other hand,

♠ K Q 8 5 3 2   ♡ Q J 3   ◊ Q 2   ♣ Q 3

is a twelve point hand that should be opened with a weak two spade bid. Remember, a non-vulnerable weak two bid should not contain more than about ten high card points. The difference between the two is that the first hand contains two control cards outside the trump suit (the king of hearts and the ace of clubs) while the second hand contains no control cards outside the trump suit. In any case, where two outside control cards are present, the weak two bidder's hand must never contain a singleton since the hand would then be too strong aggressively. Exception: A vulnerable weak two bid might be made with two control cards, a "minimum strength" suit and no intermediate cards in the outside suits. Examples of these hands are:

(a) ♠ Q J 10 9 6 5   (b) ♠ Q 10 9 7 5 4   (c) ♠ K J 9 7 5 2
    ♥ K 5 2   ♥ A 4 3   ♥ 5 4 3
    ♦ K 5   ♦ K 3   ♦ K 2
    ♣ 3 2   ♣ 3 2   ♣ K 2

D. IDEALLY, THE HAND SHOULD NOT CONTAIN A VOID.

When playing weak two bids, your partner has a right to expect a "disciplined" hand that is capable not only of attack, but of defense. We will learn in the next chapter that the partner of the weak two bidder becomes the "captain" and determines the potential of the partnership. Yet, how would you feel if you elect to open a weak two heart bid on:

   ♠ - - - -   ♥ K Q J 9 8 7   ♦ K J 9 2   ♣ 10 8 3

and your partner doubles a two spade overcall? Certainly, not as secure as if you had a doubleton, even a singleton, spade. Another reason for the taboo of any 6-4-3-0 distribution is that the bid preempts partner as well as the opponents, since we have excellent support for two suits aside from our own six card suit.

Ideal distribution, therefore, for a weak two bid is a six card suit, two doubletons, and a tripleton, or a six card suit, two tripletons, and a singleton. A six card suit, a four card minor, a doubleton and a singleton is acceptable, though slightly inferior to the 6-3-2-2 or the 6-3-3-1, due to the possible four card support for partner's minor, if he should happen to have length in that suit.

E. PREFERABLY, THE WEAK TWO BIDDER'S HAND SHOULD NOT CONTAIN AN OUTSIDE FOUR CARD MAJOR.

Holding a four card major on the side is particularly bad, since partner may have a perfect fit with your four card suit, and no fit with your six card suit. As an example, suppose you have opened the bidding with a weak two diamond bid on:

   ♠ K 5 3 2   ♥ J 7   ♦ A Q 10 7 5 3   ♣ 5

Armed with the knowledge that you have less than an opening bid, partner will pass with:

   ♠ A 10 7 5 4   ♥ K Q 5 2   ♦ 4   ♣ J 4 2

The two diamond contract is in jeopardy while four spades is almost ironclad.

A void would be even more disastrous, since not only would we have a four card major side suit, but we would have aggressive trick-taking potential that our partner could not expect, and therefore not include in his evaluation of the partnership's resources, causing competitive decisions to become impossible.

F. THE WEAK TWO BID IN THIRD AND FOURTH SEATS

As a general exception to the principles we've been discussing, distributional liberties may be taken with the weak two bid opposite a passed partner because even if a fit exists in opener's suit or a side suit, game is unlikely. This concept is exceedingly important, for if there is no game, partner should not "punish" us for our actions. He should realize that a weak two bid, especially in third seat, is often either a tactical effort to prevent the opponents from a smooth exchange of information, or lead-directing. It is important to keep in mind as we discuss the liberties that may be taken in third and fourth seat that this does not in any way negate the principles that apply to a weak two bid in first or second seat. It simply expands our perception of the value of the weak two.

THE WEAK TWO BID IN THIRD SEAT

Whenever you violate a rule in bridge there has to be a good reason for doing so. In the case of the weak two bid, you may open a good five card suit or even a hand with distribution such as 5-5-2-1 for lead directing purposes. Thus, any of the following hands would qualify for a third seat weak two bid, but would not qualify for a first or second seat weak two bid due to either suit length or general distribution:

(a) ♠ A K Q J 5	(b) ♠ 9 6 4 3 2	(c) ♠ A K Q J
♡ 8 5 4 2	♡ 5	♡ 9 4 3 2
◇ 5 3 2	◇ A K J 4 2	◇ 6 5
♣ 6	♣ 5 3	♣ 8 5 2

Hand (a) would not be acceptable in first or second position because of the five card suit (rather than six). Hand (b) is a bit eccentric in any position, because of the five card suit plus the forbidden distributional pattern, but could be opened in third seat for lead directional purposes. Hand (c) is close to a psychic weak two bid, yet, if we think about it, will probably work out more often than not, since your possession of the top honors in your suit makes it unlikely that either opponent will sit for a penalty double, and therefore you get a lead directional bid for "free." Like fine wine,

17

this sort of weak two bid should be used sparingly, only at favorable vulnerability, and with an understanding and proficient partner. Still, if you examine the equities, and see that almost any lead by partner except a spade probably would prove disastrous, the tactical reasons for the bid seem to explain themselves.*

THE WEAK TWO BID IN FOURTH SEAT

The one fact to remember when opening a weak two bid in fourth position is that you do have the alternative of passing the hand out. It is therefore incumbent upon the opener to have a reasonably good suit and a reasonably good hand. In other words, all things being equal, you should expect to have a good chance of making your partial and if partner has a "super-fitting" hand a game should not be completely out of the question. Examples of proper fourth seat weak two bids are:

(a) ♠ A K Q 8 5 4	(b) ♠ A 5 4	(c) ♠ K Q 4
♡ Q 6 4	♡ K Q J 5 3 2	♡ Q J 10 5 4 2
◇ 9 6	◇ 9 6 2	◇ 7
♣ 4 2	♣ 7	♣ K 5 3

Notice that in each case the six card suit is playable opposite very meager support and in addition there are defensive values available in case the opponents compete. Note that in each case there might be some trepidation about opening the bid at the one level, since we lack strong defensive values (2 defensive tricks) and have definite reason to fear that the opponents might enter the bidding. By opening with a weak two bid we make competition by the opponents much more hazardous.

Examples of hands that you might consider opening with a weak two bid in first, second or third position, but should not open in fourth seat are:

(a) ♠ A Q 10 5 4 3	(b) ♠ A 8 4	(c) ♠ 5 3
♡ 8	♡ K 10 8 7 4 3	♡ Q 6
◇ 7 4 2	◇ J 4	◇ A K J 5 3 2
♣ 9 8 4	♣ J 4	♣ 8 4 2

*While we definitely do not recommend a weak two bid with a four card suit to the player who is not familiar with all of the nuances of the bid, we simply could not pass up the opportunity to show the sort of creativity that is possible within the framework of the weak two bid structure.

With hand (a) the suit is adequate but the hand is too weak. Clearly with six high card points and partner a passed hand, the balance of power must belong to the opponents, so why not just pass the hand out? Hand (b) is adequate in high cards, certainly but the suit is quite poor. If we open the bidding with a weak two heart bid, we rate to go minus. Again, it would pay to pass the hand out. Hand (c) is strange since although we have a good suit and enough HCPs,* the recommended action is to pass the hand out. The reason for this is quite simple: With so few cards in the major suits, the opponents will almost surely outbid you, and if their hands are unbalanced, they may even have a game. There is no reason to court trouble by opening a weak fourth seat two bid in diamonds with both major suits inadequately protected.

* * *

To summarize, remember that the strength of the weak two bid lies in its accuracy. There are tools by which partner can find out the exact strength of your hand if he is interested, but only if you remain within the framework of the specified guidelines. The weak two bid is not only designed to cut the enemy's lines of communications, but it is also useful as a progressive and sensible bidding tool.

─────────
*HCP - High Card Points

QUIZ ON CHAPTER ONE

YOU AND YOUR PARTNER have agreed to play weak two bids. You are South and dealer. What is your opening bid on each hand?

1. Vul: 0
   ♠ Q 7
   ♡ K J 9 7 5 2
   ♢ A 5 3
   ♣ 10 7

2. Vul: N-S
   ♠ K Q 10 5 3 2
   ♡ J 7 3
   ♢ 7 2
   ♣ J 3

3. Vul: E-W
   ♠ K 4
   ♡ Q J 10
   ♢ 3 2
   ♣ K J 10 9 8 6

4. Vul: N-S
   ♠ K 7 3
   ♡ K Q 10 5 4 2
   ♢ Q 10 7
   ♣ 5

5. Vul: 0
   ♠ A K 10 8 7 2
   ♡ A J 3
   ♢ 4 3 2
   ♣ 10

6. Vul: E-W
   ♠ Q J 10 9 7 2
   ♡ 5 4 3
   ♢ J 4
   ♣ Q 5

7. Vul: Both
   ♠ J 5 3
   ♡ 4 2
   ♢ A K Q 10 5 2
   ♣ 7 3

8. Vul: E-W
   ♠ - - - -
   ♡ A Q J 10 7 5 3
   ♢ K 10 9
   ♣ 7 3 2

YOUR PARTNER DEALT and passed, and your right hand opponent passed. What is your call on each of the following hands? (You are South.)

9. Vul: 0
  ♠ K Q J 10 9 7
  ♡ J 7 5 3
  ◊ Q 7
  ♣ 8

10. Vul: Both
  ♠ 5 2
  ♡ A K Q 7 5
  ◊ Q 10 9 8
  ♣ J 8

11. Vul: E-W
  ♠ Q 10 9 7 4 2
  ♡ 8
  ◊ A Q 10
  ♣ 4 3 2

12. Vul: N-S
  ♠ A K 10 9 8 7
  ♡ K J 9 7
  ◊ 5 3
  ♣ 3

13. Vul: 0
  ♠ K Q 5 4 3 2
  ♡ A 5
  ◊ Q 4 3
  ♣ 10 7

14. Vul: N-S
  ♠ J 9 7
  ♡ K Q 9 8 5 2
  ◊ J 7 2
  ♣ 9

15. Vul: E-W
  ♠ Q J 10 8 7 5 2
  ♡ Q 2
  ◊ K 5 2
  ♣ 7

ANSWERS TO QUIZ ON CHAPTER ONE

YOU AND YOUR PARTNER have agreed to play weak two bids. You are South and dealer. What is your opening bid on each hand?

1. Vul: 0
♠ Q 7
♡ K J 9 7 5 2
◊ A 5 3
♣ 10 7

TWO HEARTS. This is a perfect weak two bid: ten high card points including one control card (the ace of diamonds) plus a suit that should play with only one loser opposite A x or Q x.

2. Vul: N-S
♠ K Q 10 5 3 2
♡ J 7 3
◊ 7 2
♣ J 3

PASS. Although the spade suit is more than adequate for a weak two bid, it is inadvisable to open with a weak two bid on less than nine high card points (including a side suit control) at unfavorable vulnerability. This hand has no winners in the side suits and if the cards do not sit well or if partner does not have a favorable hand, the opponents can double for a large penalty.

3. Vul: E-W
♠ K 4
♡ Q J 10
◊ 3 2
♣ K J 10 9 8 6

PASS. Remember that the weak two bid can be made only in diamonds, hearts, or spades. Two clubs is an artificial bid reserved for strong hands.

4. Vul: N-S
♠ K 7 3
♡ K Q 10 5 4 2
◊ Q 10 7
♣ 5

TWO HEARTS. This is a fine vulnerable weak two bid: ten high card points including a control card (the king of spades) and a fine heart suit. Compare the potential trick taking power of this hand with hand 2 and notice the difference in "texture."

5. Vul: 0
♠ A K 10 8 7 2
♡ A J 3
◊ 4 3 2
♣ 10

ONE SPADE. This hand is a trifle too strong for a weak two bid. Rule (B) specifies that the range should be from 6 to 12 points, with 12 as a decision point. In this hand, the spade suit is independent and there is admirable support if partner can bid hearts. The hand counts out to 15 points -- -- twelve high card points, one point for the sixth trump and two points for the singleton.

6. Vul: E-W

♠ Q J 10 9 7 2
♡ 5 4 3
◇ J 4
♣ Q 5

TWO SPADES. This is a poor hand and should be opened only at favorable vulnerability. Here, the two spade bid serves the dual purpose of suggesting a sacrifice and of blocking the opponents' communications. If partner has a good hand, spades is probably the proper contract anyway.

7. Vul: Both

♠ J 5 3
♡ 4 2
◇ A K Q 10 5 2
♣ 7 3

TWO DIAMONDS. The absence of outside strength is made up for by the superb quality of the diamond suit. A minimum opening bid in partner's hand may produce nine tricks in no trump.

8. Vul: E-W

♠ ----
♡ A Q J 10 7 5 3
◇ K 10 9
♣ 7 3 2

FOUR HEARTS. This hand has too much trick taking power and too little defense for a weak two bid. In addition, the spade void is highly undesirable for a weak two bid.

YOUR PARTNER DEALT and passed, and your right hand opponent passed. What is your call on each of the following hands? (You are South.)

9. Vul: 0

♠ K Q J 10 9 7
♡ J 7 5 3
◇ Q 7
♣ 8

TWO SPADES. Normally, we do not open a weak two bid with a four card major as a side suit, but, since partner is a passed hand, game is unlikely, and the weak two gives us a chance to score a partial.

10. Vul: Both

♠ 5 2
♡ A K Q 7 5
◇ Q 10 9 8
♣ J 8

TWO HEARTS. We open a weak two bid with a five card suit only if the suit is very good and the hand is close to a maximum. This action is acceptable only opposite a passed partner, when game is not likely. Here, the two heart bid is not only tactically correct, since the opponents may have a good fit in spades, but will also get partner off to the best lead if the opponents take the contract.

11. Vul: E-W

♠ Q 10 9 7 4 2
♡ 8
◇ A Q 10
♣ 4 3 2

TWO SPADES. There is a strong likelihood that left hand opponent has a good hand, and the singleton heart is cause for alarm. If your left hand opponent has only a minimum opener, you have presented him with a difficult decision.

12. Vul: N-S

♠ A K 10 9 8 7
♡ K J 9 7
◇ 5 3
♣ 3

ONE SPADE. This should be opened with a one bid, since, despite partner's pass in first seat, game is not impossible. The spot cards in spades and hearts are quite good; if partner has a fit with either major, a most optimistic view should be taken. Partner might have a hand such as

♠ Q x x   ♡ Q 10   ◇ A x x x x   ♣ J x x x

in which case four spades should be cold.

13. Vul: 0

♠ K Q 5 4 3 2
♡ A 5
◇ Q 4 3
♣ 10 7

TWO SPADES. This hand contains the same number of high card points as hand 12, yet game is unlikely because of the differences in distribution and the texture of the suits. This concept of "texture" is a key point in determining whether to open with a one bid or a weak two bid on an eleven or twelve point hand, especially in third or fourth position.

14. Vul: N-S

♠ J 9 7
♡ K Q 9 8 5 2
◇ J 7 2
♣ 9

PASS. As in hand 2, this hand is too weak to open with a weak two bid at unfavorable vulnerability. A penalty double by the enemy might prove costly.

15. Vul: E-W

♠ Q J 10 8 7 5 2
♡ Q 2
◇ K 5 2
♣ 7

THREE SPADES. With a hand as defensively weak as this one, the opportunity of blocking the opponents' communications with the seven card suit should not be missed. Here, the weak two bid is not sufficiently descriptive.

Chapter 2

RESPONSES AND REBIDS

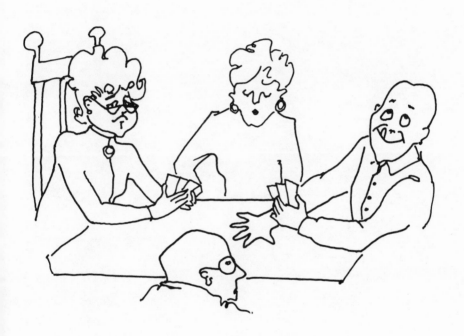

2

IN CHAPTER I WE DISSECTED THE ANATOMY of the weak two bid. We discovered that there are some very real and definite rules that restrict the use of the weak two bid to certain well-defined hand patterns. The reward for this discipline now begins to bear fruit because partner can now explore the resources of the combined hands with a remarkable degree of accuracy. There are three general categories of responses to the weak two bid:

        (A)   The new suit.
        (B)   The direct raise.
        (C)   Two no trump.

A. THE NEW SUIT

One of the basic rules of bidding is that a new suit bid by an unpassed hand is forcing for one round. This rule applies as well to the weak two bid.* If an unpassed partner bids a new suit, the weak two bidder is expected to respond in a descriptive fashion. With either a small tripleton or a doubleton ace, king or queen the weak two bidder should raise partner's suit. Thus, with:

    ♠ Q 3   ♡ A Q 10 9 8 4   ◇ J 10 2   ♣ 10 9

you open two hearts, partner responds two spades. You should raise to three spades because of your doubleton honor.

With no support in partner's suit you rebid your own suit or bid two no trump, depending on the structure of the hand. With a hand strong in intermediate cards outside the trump suit, rebid no trump.

_____

*Some partnerships modify this rule by stating that a new suit is forcing only at the two level. Thus, if one opens two hearts a response of two spades is forcing, three clubs or three diamonds is not forcing.

For instance, with:

♠ 9 2   ♡ A Q 10 7 5 2   ◊ Q 10 2   ♣ Q 4

you open two hearts -- if partner responds with two spades your rebid should be two no trump, since the hand contains good cards outside the trump suit and poor spade support. On the other hand,
suppose you open two hearts on:

♠ 9 2   ♡ A K J 9 4 2   ◊ 5 3 2   ♣ Q 2

and partner responds with two spades. This hand is weak outside
the heart suit, and the only way to show this is to rebid your hearts.
Remember, the reason partner has introduced a new suit is to investigate a possible fit for a game contract. It is the duty of the
weak two bidder to describe his hand as accurately as possible in
relation to this new suit.

B.   THE DIRECT RAISE

The direct raise of the weak two bid is never an exploratory bid.
Whenever the trump suit is raised directly, it is a request for the
weak two bidder to pass, no matter what his hand may be. For instance, suppose that you have opened the auction with two spades
and partner responds with four spades. His hand may be as good
as:

♠ Q 2   ♡ A K 5 2   ◊ A 10 9 8   ♣ K J 2

in which case he is "bidding to make." On the other hand, his hand
might be as weak as:

♠ K 5 3 2   ♡ 7   ◊ A 5 4 3 2   ♣ 7 3 2

in which case he is continuing the preempt to crowd the auction and
make communication between the opponents even more difficult.
Note that everyone is in the dark except for responder, but since
the weak two bidder is barred from bidding, the darkness affects
only the opposition. The same principle of the direct raise barring
the weak two bidder applies even in competition. For instance,
suppose the auction goes: Two spades, and the left hand opponent
makes a take-out double. Third hand holds:

♠ K 3   ♡ A 10 9 2   ◊ A 10 3 2   ♣ Q 7 2

There isn't enough for game, since the weak two bidder is known
not to have an opening bid, but responder should bid three spades
anyway as a combination preemptive and trapping bid. Three spades
should have a good chance to make and responder can double if
the enemy bids either red suit at the four level. Note that respon-

28

der may bid three spades with confidence since he knows that his partner will not bid again.

C. TWO NO TRUMP

The two no trump response is the most delicate of exploratory bids. It requires the weak two bidder to define his hand.

1. FEATURES. The most popular method of defining the hand is to show a feature as a rebid. A feature consists of a high card (ace or king) outside the trump suit. If there is no feature to show, the weak two bidder rebids his suit unless the suit is absolutely solid (A K Q x x x or better), in which case he bids three no trump, indicating that he expects to provide six tricks from his hand. The basic advantage in rebidding an ace or a king is that partner can very often place the contract in game based on a "magic fit." For instance, assume partner has opened the bidding with a weak two spade bid. You and partner have agreed to show "Features" in response to two no trump, and you elect to bid two no trump, since your hand is close to the game range. In each case partner responds three diamonds. Examine each of the following hands and determine your next action in the light of his response:

(a) ♠ Q 4   (b) ♠ Q 4   (c) ♠ Q 4
    ♡ Q J 7 6 4   ♡ J 8 5   ♡ A 5 4
    ◇ J 8 5   ◇ Q J 7 6 4   ◇ K J 10 7 6
    ♣ A K 3   ♣ A K 3   ♣ A K 3

On the first hand you should, having heard your partner show a feature (ace or king) in the diamond suit, simply return to three spades, which requests him to pass. Your 13 points plus partner's weak two bid gives you inadequate count for game unless the hands fit very well. In this case they do not, since partner has denied high cards in hearts, which is your long suit, and which would have to be set up to make game. Note the difference between hand (a) and hand (b). The hands are identical except that in hand (b) possession of a high diamond honor gives partner a good chance to produce ten tricks if his heart holding is not completely disastrous. Partner's hand might be:

   ♠ A K 7 6 5 3   ♡ 9 2   ◇ K 2   ♣ 9 7 6

in which case four spades would depend basically on no more than a 3-2 trump break. For this reason, you should bid four spades directly. Notice that possession of hand (a) would provide a very

29

poor play for game indeed, wherein hand (b) has a good chance for game. Hand (c) is a good 17 point hand and basically we need a minimum of encouragement to bid a game. That game should be in the spade suit since partner's announcement of a diamond feature leaves the heart suit wide open and partner's spades are not solid. Three no trump might be in jeopardy and four spades should be quite cold. As an example, suppose the weak two bidder has the following:

    ♠ A J 10 5 3 2   ♡ 6 2   ◊ A 9 3   ♣ 7 2

With the spade finesse on, it would be a matter of locating the queen of diamonds to make twelve tricks in spades, while three no trump would be in severe jeopardy with an opening heart lead, if the king of spades should prove to be offside. If, in hand (c) partner had shown a heart feature (which would have to be the king of hearts), then three no trump would most probably be the right bid, to protect the tenace in the diamond suit. The main rule to remember when bidding two no trump to find out about a weak two bidder's feature is that, on the "close to game" hands, (those hands where you have a minimum range opening bid opposite partner's weak two bid), the most important thing is to establish a fit with partner's feature to make up for what is most probably inadequate high card points. On the other hand, a hand of greater than minimum range opening bid count needs the merest hint of encouragement from the weak two bidder to reach a game contract. Here, the only problem is choosing which game contract to play. In any case, the two no trump bid should not be used without some sort of a fit, no matter how sparse, with partner's long suit. This is quite important, since even quite a good hand loses a great deal in value with a singleton or void in partner's suit.

    2. OGUST. Another method of rebidding over the two no trump response is called the Ogust convention. Ogust is not as simple as Features, but tends to give a more accurate description of the hand. There are five possible rebids:

    (a). With a minimum range hand in high cards, plus a poor suit the weak two bidder rebids three clubs. Hands on which you might rebid three clubs are:

♠ A J 6 4 3 2	♠ J 6 4	♠ K J 6 4 3 2
♡ Q 9 6	♡ Q 10 9 8 5 3	♡ K 5 3
◊ 7 4	◊ Q J 5	◊ 4
♣ 4 3	♣ 4	♣ 9 8 6

    (b). With a minimum range hand in high cards plus a good though not solid suit, the weak two bidder rebids three diamonds. Hands on which you might rebid three diamonds are:

♠ A Q 10 9 6 4	♠ 7 6	♠ K Q J 10 5 4
♡ Q 6 4 3	♡ A K J 10 8 6	♡ 5 3 2
◊ 8	◊ 5 3 2	◊ Q 4
♣ 5 3	♣ 8 6	♣ J 3

(c). With a maximum range hand in high cards plus a poor suit the weak two bidder rebids three hearts. Hands on which you might rebid three hearts are:

open 1S

♠ A Q 6 4 3 2	♠ A 4	♠ K Q 9 5 4 2
♡ K 9 8	♡ K J 9 7 5 4	♡ K 2
◊ Q 3	◊ Q 6 4 3	◊ Q 9 7
♣ 5 3 2	♣ 9	♣ Q 3

(d). With a maximum range hand in high cards plus a good suit the weak two bidder rebids three spades. Hands on which you might rebid three spades are:

open 1D rebid 2D

♠ 5 2 *open 1H*	♠ A 7 4	♠ K 5 3
♡ A K J 8 4 3	♡ 8 6	♡ Q 9 6
◊ K 5 3	◊ A Q J 4 3 2	◊ K Q J 10 7 4
♣ J 4	♣ 7 3	♣ 6

(e). With a solid suit (A K Q x x x) or better, the weak two bidder rebids three no trump for the same reason as in Features -- to show the ability to take six tricks in no trump.

A good way to remember these responses is that a minimum strength hand is shown with the minor suit rebids and a maximum strength hand is shown with the majors. The strong suit is shown with the highest-ranking minor or major respectively.

An interesting note is that the rebid tends to relate directly to the vulnerability. For instance, suppose an opening bid of two hearts is made on:

　　　♠ K 7　　♡ A Q 10 9 8 4　　◊ 9 8 2　　♣ 3 2

and partner responds two no trump. The partnership has agreed to play Ogust and the weak two bidder must evaluate his hand. At any vulnerability the suit is good but, as to the high card content, the hand is a maximum not vulnerable, and minimum vulnerable, since a non-vulnerable weak two bid ranges between six and ten high card points while a vulnerable weak two bid ranges between nine and twelve high card points. Therefore, non-vulnerable this weak two bidder would rebid three spades, showing a maximum high card range and a good suit, while vulnerable this same weak

31

two bidder would rebid three diamonds showing a minimum high card range and a good suit.

The following diagram should serve as an aid to the evaluation of a weak two bid when making Ogust rebids:

	HIGH CARD POINTS		SUIT
	Not Vulnerable	Vulnerable	
Minimum Range	⟨5⟩ 6-8	*good* ~~9-10~~ ⟨7⟩ 8-9 ↓ *AKxxxx*	Two out of five top cards, headed by the king or ace (occasionally the queen, with good "spot cards")
Maximum Range	*good* ⟨8⟩ 9-10 *8-9*	~~11-12~~ *10-11*	Two out of three top honors plus a jack or ten.
SOLID SUIT			Three out of three top honors.

The diagram should be self-explanatory. Not vulnerable a minimum range is six to eight HCP, the maximum is nine to ten HCP. Vulnerable, the minimum is nine to ten HCP and maximum is eleven to twelve HCP.

At any vulnerability, the minimum suit must contain two out of the five top cards in the suit. This minimum suit must be headed by the queen at least, since a suit missing the ace, king and queen makes entering the auction much too dangerous. A maximum range suit must contain two out of the three top honors (AK, KQ or KQ) plus a jack or a ten. Three out of three top honors (AKQ) would be a solid suit, admirably suited for no trump.

Now that we have established a nodding acquaintance with most of the methods of response, what sort of hand should we respond with in the first place?

With a good trump fit, it is usually politic to respond no matter what the high card strength may be, since the defensive potential is reduced by your long trumps. Let us suppose you're unfortunate enough to be dealt:

♠ K 5 3 2 ♡ 7 4 2 ◊ K J 9 7 5 ♣ 2

Your partner opened with a non-vulnerable weak two spade bid, and there you are! It does not take much imagination to realize that the enemy is certainly cold for game and may even be cold for slam. Your duty is to make communications as difficult as possible by bidding four spades. You will certainly be doubled, but the loss cannot be nearly as severe as the loss that would be incurred if the opponents reached their natural contract unencumbered.

Partner may even have opened a weak two bid on:

♠ Q J 10 9 8 4 ♡ 3 ◊ A 3 2 ♣ 9 8 4

in which case, the opposition can make at least five hearts or five clubs while your partner will make four spades in a walk if he finds the queen of diamonds. As a general rule, if you know that the hand belongs to the enemy, preempt as high as you think logically safe. Then stay out of any further bidding! Remember, any hand with good trumps is worth a bid, and sometimes partner surprises you by making the contract.

Without a trump fit: As a general rule of thumb, the less you have in the way of a trump fit, the more you need in high cards to respond. The most marginal of opening bids, with a fit, has a good chance to produce a game, because distributional points will usually make up the difference. Without a trump fit, the distributional points may well work against you. For instance, let us suppose that partner opens a weak two spade bid and you are holding:

♠ 2 ♡ A Q 9 8 ◊ A Q 10 2 ♣ K 10 4 3

This is a good fifteen point hand, but the singleton spade is a deficit. The recommended response is a pass. While it is possible that all the finesses will work and all the suits will break and you may make a lucky game contract, the hands do not fit well, and the likelihood is that game is not makable. Another reason for passing is that if the opposition decides to enter the bidding, you will be able to punish them for their impertinence by doubling anything on the three level.

In Chapter IV, we will go into "tactical" responses and rebids or how to make life even more difficult for the opponents. For the moment, turn to Quiz II to solidify the weak two bid knowledge you have acquired.

QUIZ ON CHAPTER TWO

IN EACH PROBLEM, YOU ARE SOUTH. Partner opens the bidding with a weak two heart bid. Your right hand opponent passes. What is your call? (You and your partner are playing Ogust responses.)

1. Vul: N-S
   ♠ K 5 3 2
   ♡ 2
   ◊ A K Q 2
   ♣ J 10 3 2

2. Vul: E-W
   ♠ 5
   ♡ 9 4 3 2
   ◊ 7 6 4 2
   ♣ A 10 7 3

3. Vul: Both
   ♠ A K 3
   ♡ K 10 2
   ◊ A Q 4 3 2
   ♣ 3 2

4. Vul: E-W
   ♠ A Q 10
   ♡ A 3
   ◊ J 9 8 4
   ♣ J 10 7 4

5. Vul: Both
   ♠ K Q 10
   ♡ 7 3
   ◊ K Q 9 7
   ♣ K 4 3 2

6. Vul: N-S
   ♠ A J 9 7 6 5
   ♡ 8
   ◊ A J 10 3
   ♣ K 4

AS SOUTH, YOU HAVE OPENED THE BIDDING with two spades. Partner responds two no trump. You and your partner have agreed to play Ogust responses. What is your call? (The opponents pass throughout.) If you and your partner had agreed to play Features instead of Ogust, what would you bid?

7. Vul: N-S
   ♠ K Q 10 9 7 4
   ♡ K 5
   ◊ J 9 8
   ♣ 5 3

8. Vul: Both
   ♠ A Q 10 7 3 2
   ♡ K Q 4
   ◊ 9 7 2
   ♣ 2

9. Vul: E-W
   ♠ K Q J 7 6 2
   ♡ K 7 3
   ◊ J 3
   ♣ 8 2

10. Vul: N-S
    ♠ A K Q J 4 2
    ♡ 3 2
    ◊ 9 7 2
    ♣ 8 7

11. Vul: 0
    ♠ Q 10 6 5 4 2
    ♡ A J 3
    ◊ J 3 2
    ♣ 2

12. Vul: Both
    ♠ Q J 10 9 8 7
    ♡ A Q
    ◊ Q J 3
    ♣ 7 4

don't open 2 with 12 ACP

YOUR PARTNER, NORTH, OPENS THE BIDDING with two hearts. You respond two no trump, initiating the Ogust convention. In each example, what is your call after the indicated rebid by partner?

13. Vul: N-S
    N: 3♡
    ♠ Q 10 9 2
    ♡ Q 4
    ◊ A Q 7 6
    ♣ K 10 2

14. Vul: E-W
    N: 3♣
    ♠ A 7 2
    ♡ K 2
    ◊ A J 3 2
    ♣ Q 7 4 2

15. Vul: Both
    N: 3NT
    ♠ A 2
    ♡ 3 2
    ◊ A K Q J 10
    ♣ A 7 3 2

16. Vul: 0
    N: 3♠
    ♠ K Q
    ♡ K 9 3
    ◊ A K J 10 7 6 4
    ♣ 2

17. Vul: E-W
    N: 3◊
    ♠ A 10 2
    ♡ Q 5 4 3
    ◊ A 10 3
    ♣ K 7 2

18. Vul: 0
    N: 3NT
    ♠ 9 7 2
    ♡ 4
    ◊ A Q J 9
    ♣ A K J 5 2

19. Vul: E-W
    N: 3♣
    ♠ A K 2
    ♡ Q 7 3
    ◊ A 5 4 3
    ♣ A J 9

20. Vul: 0
    N: 3NT
    ♠ K 2
    ♡ 5 4 3
    ◊ A K 6 4 2
    ♣ A 3 2

NOW LET'S ADD SOME SPICE! You are South and your partner opens the bidding with two diamonds. The enemy competes with the indicated overcall. What is your bid?

21. Vul: Both
    Opp: 2♠
    ♠ K 10 8 4
    ♡ A Q 10 4
    ◊ 2
    ♣ A K 9 7

22. Vul: E-W
    Opp: Dbl.
    ♠ Q J 9 7 4
    ♡ Q J 10 4
    ◊ ----
    ♣ K 7 6 3

23. Vul: E-W
    Opp: Dbl.
    ♠ 2
    ♡ A 6 4 3 2
    ◊ K 9 7 3
    ♣ 7 6 3

24. Vul: N-S
    Opp: 4♡
    ♠ Q 5 2
    ♡ J 7 3
    ◇ 9 8 7 3
    ♣ K 6 2

25. Vul: E-W
    Opp: 3◇
    ♠ A K
    ♡ 3 2
    ◇ J 9 8 7 3 2
    ♣ 5 4 2

26. Vul: Both
    Opp: 2NT
    ♠ A 7 3 2
    ♡ Q 10 3 2
    ◇ 9 7 2
    ♣ Q 2

27. Vul: E-W
    Opp: Dbl.
    ♠ Q J 9 7
    ♡ K Q 9 2
    ◇ Q 7 4
    ♣ J 2

28. Vul: Both
    Opp: 3♡
    ♠ A J 7 5 2
    ♡ A 9 7
    ◇ K 7 3 2
    ♣ 5

ANSWERS TO QUIZ ON CHAPTER TWO

IN EACH PROBLEM, YOU ARE SOUTH. Partner opens the bidding with a weak two heart bid. Your right hand opponent passes. What is your call? (You and your partner are playing Ogust responses.)

1. Vul: N-S
♠ K 5 3 2
♡ 2
♢ A K Q 2
♣ J 10 3 2

PASS. With a minimum opening bid, you need a fit in partner's trump suit to take aggressive action. Two hearts is the best spot for a plus score, and you have adequate defense if the opponents enter the bidding. Any play for game would be tenuous at best.

2. Vul: E-W
♠ 5
♡ 9 4 3 2
♢ 7 6 4 2
♣ A 10 7 3

FOUR HEARTS. Emergency measures must be taken! Your vulnerable opponents are cold for at least a game and you are duty bound to make enemy communications as difficult as possible. Four hearts doubled should be a better result than letting the opponents get together in their spade suit.

3. Vul: Both
♠ A K 3
♡ K 10 2
♢ A Q 4 3 2
♣ 3 2

FOUR HEARTS. Compare this hand with hand #2. If the enemy attempts to enter the bidding this time, you will punish them unmercifully. This is the dilemma which faces the opponents of the weak two bidder. Are you bidding four hearts to "make" or just confounding their communications?

4. Vul: E-W
♠ A Q 10
♡ A 3
♢ J 9 8 4
♣ J 10 7 4

THREE HEARTS. Game is unlikely, and if forced to defend, you'd rather do so at a higher level. Your hand should be good enough to make three hearts.

5. Vul: Both
♠ K Q 10
♡ 7 3
♢ K Q 9 7
♣ K 4 3 2

TWO NO TRUMP. If partner has a good vulnerable weak two bid, you want to try three no trump. If partner responds three clubs, you plan to return to three hearts. A low doubleton is considered a fit in partner's suit.

6. Vul: N-S   TWO SPADES. If partner has a spade fit, you
♠ A J 9 7 6 5   will try four spades. If partner denies a spade
♡ 8   fit, let him play in three hearts. It should be as
◇ A J 10 3   good a spot as any for a part score and with no fit
♣ K 4   there is no game.

AS SOUTH, YOU HAVE OPENED THE BIDDING with two spades.
Partner responds two no trump. You and your partner have agreed
to play Ogust responses. What is your call? (The opponents pass
throughout.) If you and your partner had agreed to play Features
instead of Ogust, what would you bid?

7. Vul: N-S   THREE DIAMONDS. Vulnerable, your hand is of
♠ K Q 10 9 7 4   a minimum character in high cards and your suit
♡ K 5   is good. Not vulnerable, with the same hand, you
◇ J 9 8   should bid three spades, since the high card strength
♣ 5 3   would then be in the maximum range. (Playing
             "Features" you would bid THREE HEARTS, show-
             ing the king of hearts.)

8. Vul: Both   THREE SPADES. This is a fine weak two bid. You
♠ A Q 10 7 3 2   have eleven high card points and a good suit. Three
♡ K Q 4   spades is the response that passes on the good news
◇ 9 7 2   to your partner. Any other bid would be an under-
♣ 2   bid. (Playing "Features" you would bid THREE
             HEARTS, showing the king of hearts.)

9. Vul: E-W   THREE SPADES. Not vulnerable, this hand is
♠ K Q J 7 6 2   maximum both in high cards and in suit. Remem-
♡ K 7 3   ber, the Ogust response requirements differ with
◇ J 3   the vulnerability. This same hand would respond
♣ 8 2   three diamonds if vulnerable. If you are having
             trouble with this, refer to the chart on page 32.
             (Playing "Features" you would bid THREE HEARTS,
             showing the king of hearts.)

10. Vul: N-S   THREE NO TRUMP. This shows a solid, running
♠ A K Q J 4 2   suit in no trump, which is exactly what you have.
♡ 3 2   (Playing "Features" you would bid THREE NO
◇ 9 7 2   TRUMP, for the same reason.)
♣ 8 7

11. Vul: 0
♠ Q 10 6 5 4 2
♡ A J 3
◊ J 3 2
♣ 2

THREE CLUBS. You probably shouldn't have opened a weak two bid with a suit this weak, but having used your "poetic license" to do so, tell your partner you have nothing as quickly as possible. (Playing "Features" you would bid THREE HEARTS, showing the ace of hearts.)

open 1S

12. Vul: Both
♠ Q J 10 9 8 7
♡ A Q
◊ Q J 3
♣ 7 4

THREE HEARTS. You have a full vulnerable maximum in high cards (twelve points), but your suit does not contain the required two out of three top honors. The three heart bid tells your partner that your hand is good but your suit is bad. (Playing "Features" you would bid THREE HEARTS, showing the ace of hearts.)*

YOUR PARTNER, NORTH, OPENS THE BIDDING with two hearts. You respond two no trump, initiating the Ogust convention. In each example, what is your call after the indicated rebid by partner?

13. Vul: N-S
N: 3♡
♠ Q 10 9 2
♡ Q 4
◊ A Q 7 6
♣ K 10 2

THREE NO TRUMP. Nine tricks should be easier to make than ten. The queen of hearts should be an adequate filler for partner's suit, and in any event, you certainly want the lead coming up to your hand.

14. Vul: E-W
N: 3♣
♠ A 7 2
♡ K 2
◊ A J 3 2
♣ Q 7 4 2

THREE HEARTS. Partner is showing a minimum non-vulnerable hand (six to eight points and poor hearts). In the face of that, you must settle for a partial. There just isn't enough for game.

*Please notice that when playing "Features" we responded three hearts on five quite differently structured weak two bids (Nos. 7, 8, 9, 11, 12). This is why we prefer the more accurate Ogust convention, since it allows us to describe the general strength of a hand, together with the texture of the opener's suit, with one bid.

15. Vul: Both
N: 3NT
♠ A 2
♡ 3 2
◇ A K Q J 10
♣ A 7 3 2

SEVEN NO TRUMP. Easy as pie. Partner has shown a solid suit, so we can count six heart tricks, five diamonds, and two black aces. (It is possible that partner'ꞏ hearts are A K Q x x x and the opponents' heꞏꞏts divide 4-1, but that's a chance we have to ꞏꞏke.)

16. Vul: 0
N: 3♠
♠ K Q
♡ K 9 3
◇ A K J 10
♣ 2 \7 6 4

FOUR ꞏVO TRUMP. Your partner said he has a good hand with good hearts -- your king of hearts should ensure no heart losers. If partner's side control is an ace, bid six hearts. If you are off two aces, the hand should still be safe at the five level.

17. Vul: E-W
N: 3◇
♠ A 10 2
♡ Q 5 4 3
◇ A 10 3
♣ K 7 2

THREE NO TRUMP. Partner says he has a good suit and a bad hand. Despite the 6-4 heart fit, game should be attempted in no trump if at all. You have eight tricks to start with (six hearts and two aces). A club lead will give you a ninth trick, and if diamonds or spades are led, you may find something like J x in dummy and be able to scramble nine tricks anyway. If partner's response is accurate, four hearts is unlikely.

18. Vul: 0
N: 3NT
♠ 9 7 2
♡ 4
◇ A Q J 9
♣ A K J 5 2

FOUR HEARTS. Three no trump would be an error. Partner has a solid heart suit, but you have no spade stopper. In four hearts, the minor suit holdings should provide enough "meat and potatoes."

19. Vul: E-W
N: 3♣
♠ A K 2
♡ Q 7 3
◇ A 5 4 3
♣ A J 9

FOUR HEARTS. Too bad! If partner showed any sign of life, you would try for a slam, but in the face of a minimum rebid, slam is out of the question. You may have a trump loser and the minors are wide open.

20. Vul: 0
N: 3NT
♠ K 2
♡ 5 4 3
◊ A K 6 4 2
♣ A 3 2

PASS. No problem -- with partner's solid suit you have nine top tricks (a tenth if spades are led). A badly placed ace of spades may defeat four hearts.

NOW LET'S ADD SOME SPICE! You are South and your partner opens the bidding with two diamonds. The enemy competes with the indicated overcall. What is your bid?

21. Vul: Both
Opp: 2♠
♠ K 10 8 4
♡ A Q 10 4
◊ 2
♣ A K 9 7

DOUBLE. They are in trouble with no place to go. Your partner's weak two bid has done its duty. The partner of the overcaller probably has a delicious yarborough. You might get as much as a four or five trick set out of the hand.

22. Vul: E-W
Opp: Dbl.
♠ Q J 9 7 4
♡ Q J 10 4
◊ ----
♣ K 7 6 3

PASS. You're in a misfit -- don't try to rescue partner. Any bid you make may make the situation worse than it already is. Besides the opponents may bid something and save you.

23. Vul: E-W
Opp: Dbl.
♠ 2
♡ A 6 4 3 2
◊ K 9 7 3
♣ 7 6 3

FIVE DIAMONDS. Non-vulnerable, your duty is to crowd the auction. Five diamonds doubled does not rate to go down more than two or three, and the opponents can certainly make a vulnerable game. After your bid, they may end up in five of a major and be too high -- e.g. partner may have a singleton heart and the ace of diamonds.

24. Vul: N-S
Opp: 4♡
♠ Q 5 2
♡ J 7 3
◊ 9 8 7 3
♣ K 6 2

PASS. The opponents surely have a game, but the weaknesses in your side suits make a vulnerable sacrifice too costly against non-vulnerable opponents.

25. Vul: E-W
    Opp: 3◊
♠ A K
♡ 3 2
◊ J 9 8 7 3 2
♣ 5 4 2

SIX DIAMONDS. Bizarre, but logical, and tacti-cally sound, if you think about it! Partner's non-vulnerable weak two bid must be headed by at least two out of the top three honors since you have a twelve card fit! There isn't room in his hand for much else, so the opposition rates to be cold for any five level contract. With such an obscured auction, there is a good chance the enemy will bid a slam which you can double with alacrity. If part-ner bids seven diamonds, homicide will be justi-fied. Remember, he is barred from bidding over any direct raise or jump raise of his suit.

26. Vul: Both
    Opp: 2NT
♠ A 7 3 2
♡ Q 10 3 2
◊ 9 7 2
♣ Q 2

PASS. The diamonds lay badly for any kind of a save and you may have enough defense to beat a no trump game, since you have marginal stoppers in the other suits and three cards in diamonds for communication with partner's long suit.

27. Vul: E-W
    Opp: Dbl.
♠ Q J 9 7
♡ K Q 9 2
◊ Q 7 4
♣ J 2

THREE DIAMONDS. This is a tactical bid. Part-ner should have a play for three diamonds -- if the opponents enter the bidding you have adequate de-fense against a partial and enough to double a game contract.

28. Vul: Both
    Opp: 3♡
♠ A J 7 5 2
♡ A 9 7
◊ K 7 3 2
♣ 5

FIVE DIAMONDS. This bid is tactically correct for many reasons. Firstly, your partner is liable to make it if he has any sort of a fitting major suit holding. Secondly, you plan to double five hearts and lead the singleton club, hoping for either a dia-mond entry or a singleton spade in partner's hand to beat the contract.

43

Chapter 3

THE STRONG TWO CLUB BID

3

THE AUTHOR IS NOT ONE OF THOSE FORTUNATE PLAYERS who is dealt a great many strong two opening bids. The last time I held a strong two bid, my partner made a negative response of two no trump and we ended up playing three no trump. I don't recall if partner made the contract, but I do remember that the defense was annoyingly sharp because all my high cards were in full view of a calculating enemy. Common sense says that the strong hand should be concealed from the opposition whenever possible. The artificial strong two club opening bid conforms to the principle of keeping the strong hand concealed, and since, as we will see, a two no trump response is reserved for a good hand while two diamonds is a negative response, this bidding method provides a degree of flexibility not found in the "strong two" methods.

As stated at the start of Chapter I, the weak two bid is made in the diamond, heart or spade suits, while an opening bid of two clubs is strong, forcing, and artificial, showing the equivalent of a strong two bid in "Standard American."

There are two basic types of strong two bids. These are the "flat hand" (no trump oriented) and the distributional hand (suit oriented). After partner responds to a forcing two club bid, the two club bidder describes his hand with a rebid. Thus, with:

    ♠ A K Q J x x x   ♡ A K x   ◇ A Q J   ♣ - - -

the opening bid is two clubs and a rebid of spades shows the equivalent of a strong two spade opening bid. However, before going into the rebids and problems of the opener, let us consider the various responses open to the partner of the two club opening bidder.

POSITIVE VS. NEGATIVE RESPONSES — EVALUATION OF POINTS

There are different classes of responses. It is imperative that the difference between the positive, or forward going, hand, and the negative, or discouraging, hand be understood. This evaluation is based on high card points and controls, since distribution cannot be taken into consideration until more is known about the two club bidder's hand. For instance, a hand with a spade void would not be valuable to the two club bidder if his strong suit is spades. To consider a positive response, it is necessary to have a hand which evaluates to eight points. This evaluation process is based on high card points and on the number of controls in the responder's hand: ace-two controls, king-one control. With only one control, deduct one point from the total high card points. With no controls, deduct two points from the total high card points. With three controls, add one point to the total high card points, and with two controls, no points are added or subtracted. With an evaluated total of less than eight points, a negative response of two diamonds is made. With an evaluated total of eight or more points, a positive response is indicated. As an example, suppose partner opens two clubs and you are looking at the following hands:

(a) ♠ A 7 5 3
    ♡ Q 10 3
    ◊ 5 4 3 2
    ♣ 3 2

(b) ♠ K J 10 7
    ♡ Q 10 3
    ◊ J 5 4
    ♣ J 3 2

(c) ♠ A 7 5 3
    ♡ Q J 7
    ◊ J 10 7 4
    ♣ 9 8

(d) ♠ A 9 8 7
    ♡ K 4 3 2
    ◊ 3 2
    ♣ 4 3 2

(e) ♠ K J 5 4 3
    ♡ 2
    ◊ Q 10 9 8 4
    ♣ 3 2

(f) ♠ A 5 3 2
    ♡ A 5 4
    ◊ Q 7 6 3
    ♣ 9 7

On hand (a) you only have six high card points and even the possession of two controls (the ace of spades) does not allow you to add any points. This is therefore a negative-response hand.

On hand (b) you have eight high card points, but you must deduct a point because you only have one control (the king of spades) leaving you with seven evaluated points, which is a negative response.

In hand (c), on the other hand, you hold eight high card points with two controls, which indicates a positive response.

Hand (d) adds up to only seven high card points but with three controls (the ace of spades and the king of hearts), you can add one point, bringing the evaluated total up to eight points, which is, of course, a positive response.

With hand (e), although we have two playable five card suits and good distributional values, it is our duty to tell partner that we have less than eight evaluated points by making a negative response. Remember that distributional points do not count in the initial eval-

48

uation. For instance, if the two club bidder has a heart-club hand, our long suits would be valueless. On the other hand, if partner has a strong two bid that is either no trump oriented or has a fit in either diamonds or spades, our hand is obviously quite a bit better. We must wait and see.

Hand (f) is, of course, a positive response. We have ten high card points which revalue to twelve evaluated points based on the four controls (two for each ace), and since partner has promised the equivalent of a strong two bid, slam is certainly a very strong possibility. You will, of course, make a positive response and listen carefully to partner's description of his hand.

RESPONSES

A. TWO DIAMONDS, NEGATIVE

The two diamond bid in response to partner's two club opening bid to describe any hand with less than eight evaluated points has certain advantages which make it the single most popular method of response. First, it describes at the lowest possible level the hand which you will have most frequently opposite a strong two bid. Second, it eliminates the two no trump response to show a poor hand, allowing the stronger hand to play a no trump contract, if such is indicated. When using the two diamond negative response, any bid except two diamonds shows a hand with eight or more evaluated points and is, of course, forcing to game.

B. A SUIT BID (OTHER THAN TWO DIAMONDS)

This shows a hand with eight or more evaluated points, plus a five card suit headed by at least one honor. As an example, suppose partner opens two clubs and you are looking at the following hands:

(a) ♠ A J 6 4 3 (b) ♠ J 5 3 (c) ♠ A J 4 (d) ♠ K Q 5 4 3 2
    ♡ K 8 3   ♡ K Q 10 3 2   ♡ 5 3   ♡ 8 7
    ◊ 8 5 2   ◊ K 8 6   ◊ K 10 9 4 2   ◊ 4
    ♣ 8 6   ♣ 4 2   ♣ 8 7 5   ♣ J 9 6 2

Hand (a) contains nine evaluated points (eight in high cards plus an extra point for three controls), and a good five card spade suit. Therefore, the indicated response to your partner's strong two club

49

bid is two spades. With hand (b) two hearts is the correct response with your good five card suit and your nine evaluated points. On hand (c) the correct response is three diamonds. Notice that two diamonds would be incorrect, since that would describe a hand with less than eight evaluated points and would say nothing about the diamond suit. Here we have a good five card diamond suit and nine evaluated points (eight in high cards and one for the third control). On hand (d) we must respond two diamonds despite our excellent six card spade suit. The subsequent auction may indicate that partner can support our spades, in which case we may bid quite vigorously, but for the present it is our duty to tell partner that we do not have enough in high card strength to make a positive response.

C. THE NO TRUMP RESPONSE TO THE STRONG TWO CLUB BID

In general, this shows a "flat hand" (no singletons or voids) with eight or more evaluated points. The number of no trump with which we respond is dependent directly upon the point count. Thus, if partner opens two clubs, and we have eight to ten evaluated points, the response is two no trump. With eleven to thirteen evaluated points, the response is three no trump. As an example, suppose partner opens two clubs and you have each of the following hands:

(a) ♠ A 10 3   (b) ♠ K J 5 3   (c) ♠ Q J 5   (d) ♠ A 10 7 5
    ♡ K 9 3 2   ♡ A 6 4 2   ♡ K 7 6   ♡ K J 10 9
    ◊ Q 4 3   ◊ 7 5 3   ◊ Q 8 3   ◊ 3
    ♣ 6 4 2   ♣ K 2   ♣ 6 4 3 2   ♣ J 10 6 4

On hand (a) we have ten evaluated points (nine points in high cards plus a point for three controls), so the indicated response is two no trump. On hand (b) we have thirteen evaluated points (eleven in high cards plus two extra points for four controls). This hand falls into the 11-13 point range and we should bid three no trump in response to our partner's two club bid. On hand (c) we must bid two diamonds. We have eight high card points but the possession of only one control forces us to reduce our point count by one, and seven evaluated points is the negative response by our methods. Hand (d) is a problem. We have a singleton which makes bidding no trump "against the rules" and we have no five card suit to bid. Yet, we do have a positive hand. Our own preference would be to treat the excellent four card suit as a five card suit and bid two hearts. In a situation such as this, the decision whether to bid no trump with a singleton or respond with a four card suit is a matter of style, and should be based on the texture of the suit to be bid.

AN ALTERNATE SYSTEM OF RESPONSES

STEP RESPONSES: This method of responding to the strong two club opening bid is derived from European systems. Treating a king as one "control" and an ace as two "controls," the two diamond response shows zero or one control, two hearts shows two controls (one ace or two kings), two spades shows an ace and king (three controls), two no trump shows three kings (also three controls), three clubs shows four controls, and three diamonds shows five or more controls. After the initial control-showing response, the auction proceeds naturally.

THE TWO CLUB OPENER'S REBID WITH A FLAT HAND

The flat, or no trump oriented, hand is rebid strictly on the basis of the high cards. With 23 or 24 high card points, the two club opener rebids two no trump. With 25 to 27 points, the rebid is three no trump, and with 28 HCP, the two club opener rebids four no trump. The rebids are the same whether the responder shows a positive or a negative hand.

After the two club bidder has defined his point range, the responder can evaluate the future of the combined hands. Assuming that the two club bidder has rebid two no trump (23-24 HCP), responder should, with a flat hand and no distributional values:

    (a) Pass with 0-2 points.
    (b) Bid three no trump with 3-7 points.
    (c) Bid four no trump with 8 or 9 points (asking the two club bidder to bid six no trump with a maximum).
    (d) Bid six no trump with 10-12 points.
    (e) Bid five no trump with 13 points, asking the two club bidder to bid seven no trump with a maximum and six no trump with a minimum.
    (f) Bid seven no trump with 14 or more points.

With distributional values, responder can either bid three clubs (Stayman) to inquire whether the two club bidder has a four card major or show length in a suit by bidding that suit, indicating distributional values for a suit contract.

With these facts in mind, assume you are holding the following:

♠ K 9 8 7 6   ♡ K 7 3   ◊ 5 4   ♣ 9 8 6

Partner opens two clubs, you respond with a negative two diamonds (six evaluated points), and partner rebids two no trump. The proper rebid with this hand is three spades, telling partner that you have five or more spades and three to seven high card points. On the basis of this knowledge, he can make a decision whether to play three no trump or four spades. This decision is normally based on the number of spades held by the two club opener. With three or more spades he should almost always bid four spades, while with only two spades he bids three no trump (which partner will correct to four spades if he has six or more spades). Slam is out of the question, since responder has denied the values to investigate the possibility of slam. This is a good point to remember: When you open two clubs and rebid no trump, you have a nice hand, but have described it all. Responder becomes the "captain of the ship" and determines the future of the hand.

THE OPENER'S REBID WITH A DISTRIBUTIONAL HAND

This type of two club opening bid is based not only upon a multitude of high cards, but also a long suit. Basically, any hand that would be opened with a strong two bid in Standard American bidding should be opened two clubs with the intention of bidding the long suit later. Unlike the no trump oriented hand, the rebid in a suit does not limit the hand, and there is no maximum point count.

With a suit oriented two club opener, distributional points are also counted to determine if the hand is worthy of a two demand bid. Using a standard scale of awarding distributional points (three for a void, two for a singleton, one for a doubleton, one for a good six card suit, and two points for a good seven card suit, etc.), the suit oriented two club bid should consist of at least 24 points, twenty of which are in high cards. The reason for this high card point requirement is that the two club bidder should be able to control the auction. You should be within a trick of game in your own hand and able to defend if the opponents enter the bidding. Examine the following four hands:

(a)	(b)
♠ A K Q 9 7 4	♠ K Q 4
♡ A J 10	♡ A Q 7 4 2
◊ A K	◊ K Q J
♣ 7 4	♣ A Q

(c) ♠ ----	(d) ♠ ----
♡ A K Q J 10 9 8 7	♡ A K Q J 10 9 8 7
◇ K Q J x	◇ A K
♣ Q	♣ Q J 10

Hand (a) is a sound two club opening. We have 24 points, 21 in high cards, one point for each doubleton, and one point for spade length. A high club or any help in hearts makes game a virtual certainty. Hand (b) should also be opened two clubs since we have 23 HCP, but we would treat this type of hand as a flat (no trump) hand. The heart suit is not nearly good enough, and with all suits well stopped, the hand is best described by a no trump rebid. Hand (c) on the other hand should not be opened two clubs even though we have game in our own hand. The high card content is insufficient; if partner has a bad hand, the opponents might make a slam in either black suit -- an ignominious result after a two demand bid. Hand (d) is similar in structure to hand (c), but look at the difference. Here, two clubs is the right bid. A club honor makes a slam certain for our side. We have the necessary twenty high card points plus so many distributional points we can scarcely count them.

RESPONDER'S REBIDS

DOUBLE NEGATIVES

This is a fancy name for a very simple concept. Assume that partner has opened the auction with two clubs, and you have been forced to respond with a negative two diamond bid. Partner now rebids two spades. You might have a fit with a good hand -- you might have a fit with a bad hand. Likewise, you might have no fit with a good hand, or no fit and a completely useless hand for partner. It is imperative to convey this information as quickly as possible for the sake of accuracy. This is where a new technique, the double negative, comes in. Simply, it is an extension of the two diamond negative system of response. First of all, consider the case where you have a fit with partner. With a poor hand containing a trump fit, the responder jumps directly to game, while with a maximum two diamond bid and a trump fit, the responder raises the two club bidder's real suit one level. The logic of the single raise in partner's suit showing a stronger hand is that it leaves room for investigation, while the leap to game denies the desire to investigate the possibilities of slam. In the event that responder does not have a trump fit, a useless hand is described by a three club bid, otherwise known as the second negative. Any other bid shows a fair hand without a fit in partner's suit. Consider the following four hands. Partner opens the auction with two clubs and you respond two diamonds. When partner rebids two spades, showing a strong two bid in the spade suit, you have to make a bid. What call do you make with each of these hands?

(a) ♠ 6   (b) ♠ J 8 7 3   (c) ♠ Q 10 8   (d) ♠ J 3
    ♡ J 9 4   ♡ J 9 2   ♡ A 10 4   ♡ K 10 8
    ◊ J 8 6 2   ◊ 6   ◊ J 9 7 4 3   ◊ Q 10 6 4
    ♣ 7 5 4 3 2 ♣ 6 5 4 3 2 ♣ 9 8   ♣ J 9 8 3

On hand (a) the correct bid is three clubs showing a bad hand with no fit.* On hand (b) the proper call is four spades, showing a bad hand with a fit. On hand (c) the bid should be three spades, leaving room for partner to investigate a slam, since the values have been promoted by the established fit. Finally, on hand (d) a two no trump call is best, showing a "maximum negative response" without a trump fit. Partner will know that you do not have a very good hand because of your initial two diamond response. As we mentioned earlier, one of the great advantages of the double negative method is that it allows the responder to quickly describe what type of hand he holds. As an example, suppose you have:

    ♠ A K Q 10 5 3   ♡ A K   ◊ A 6 3   ♣ 6 3

You open the auction with two clubs and partner responds two diamonds. Over your two spade rebid partner bids three clubs (the second bid of the double negative). If you bid three spades (which is non-forcing), partner can pass and indeed three spades may be the limit of the hand. On the auction, partner may hold as little as:

    ♠ 6 3   ♡ 8 5 2   ◊ J 9 4 2   ♣ Q 6 4 3

in which case the jack of spades has to drop for you to be able to take nine tricks.

The last thing to consider under the category of two club openings with distributional hands are the positive responses and rebids and what to do with them. To cover these, and to complete the general structure of the strong two club bid, see the diagram on pages 56-57.

---

*If the two club opener rebids clubs as his suit, then a diamond bid becomes the second negative; if the opener rebids diamonds, then hearts become the second negative. In all cases the second negative is either clubs or the next cheapest suit available above three clubs.

To enter the "Royal Road of Responding" partner must, of course, open two clubs. We come immediately to our first crossroad -- whether we have a positive hand or a negative hand. With more than eight evaluated points we follow the "positive hand" road sign in an easterly direction. With a hand that contains less than eight evaluated points, we follow the negative hand road marker in a southerly direction. Whichever road we elect to take, partner will show his suit, and we will come to another crossroad. Let us further consider the negative road, since we are familiar with the various paths we may take by using the "double negative" method of response. With a useless hand and no fit, we would bid three clubs (or the cheapest available suit, if the bidding has passed three clubs), while with a useless hand containing a fit, we leap to game in the opener's suit. Since you have no interest in slam, but are sure that there is game, you eliminate the possibility of investigation (and misunderstanding) by bidding game directly. Please note that both these roads lead away from "Slam Town." The third and fourth roads, while they are not direct paths to the town of Slam, do not lead away from it. With a hand that increases in value due to a fit, we would raise partner's suit one level. Partner will now know that we have a fair hand, although it is limited by the original two diamond response. The other possibilities are bids of a new suit or no trump with a maximum two diamond response and no fit. Note that while the main road of these last two leads away from Slam Town to game. it is a path that can take you over to "Slam Avenue."

The crossroads on the positive path are simply a matter of fit or no fit with partner's suit. With no fit, rebid your suit or bid a new suit with a suit oriented hand, and no trump with a flat hand. With a fit, raise your partner's suit one level. Note that whichever action you take you now find yourself on Slam Avenue.

Most people who end up on Slam Avenue wouldn't think of missing a visit to Convention Hall. Here we find all the gadgets that make bridge sometimes fun and sometimes torturous. The cue bids, the asking bids, the fragment bids, the anti-fragment bids, Blackwood, Gerber, etc., etc. Here we can check the quality of trump suits and side suit length and almost anything else that we have weapons for in our bidding arsenals. Having left Convention Hall there are roads to exit at the four level and at the five level, and finally we come to Slam Town, which is a split level establishment, one called Small Slam Town and one called Grand Slam Town.

THE ROYAL ROAD TO RESPONDING TO
SUIT ORIENTED HANDS

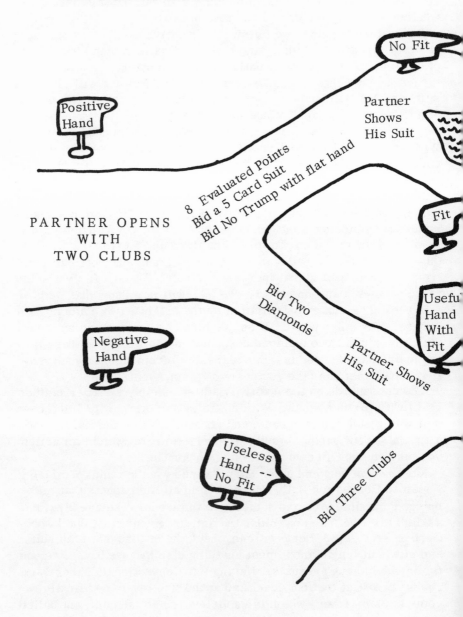

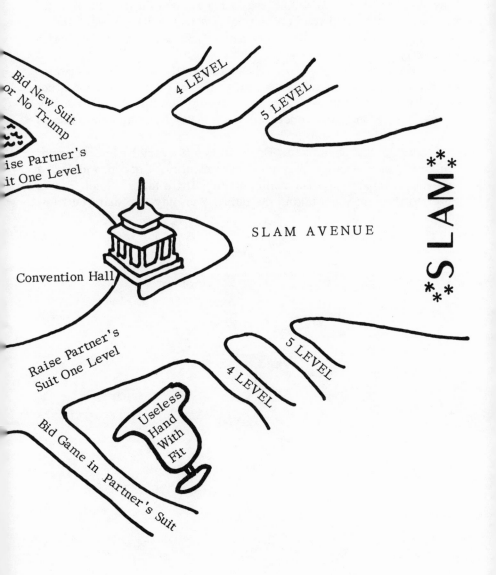

Bid New Suit
or No Trump

ise Partner's
it One Level

4 LEVEL

5 LEVEL

S LAM

SLAM AVENUE

Convention Hall

Raise Partner's
Suit One Level

5 LEVEL

4 LEVEL

Useless
Hand
With
Fit

Bid Game in Partner's Suit

This map is by no means absolute. You may elect to guide partner on one of the "useless hand" roads by your responses, and yet he may "fly" to slam. All right, that's his responsibility. Meanwhile you have discharged your obligation as a partner in setting him on what you believed to be the right path. You have bid your own cards correctly.

One thing should be clear. The strong artificial two club opening bid does not lose anything and gains the freedom to use the other three suits for weak two bids. The strong two club opening usually keeps the strong hand concealed since a two no trump response is not made with bad hands.

A note to the perplexed: Don't worry if every little fact is not embossed on a photographic plate in your mind. Concept and theory are more important than remembering little facts. Feel free to refer to the text when taking the quiz. You may find that you know more than you think.

QUIZ ON CHAPTER III

YOU ARE LOOKING AT THESE VERY GOOD HANDS. Count your points and (a) determine what to open and (b) if you elect to open a strong two club bid, what is your rebid if partner responds two diamonds?

1. ♠ A Q J 9 7 3
   ♡ A Q 8
   ◊ K J 8
   ♣ 2

2. ♠ A K Q J 7 6 2
   ♡ A K 2
   ◊ A 2
   ♣ 7

3. ♠ K J 9 7 3
   ♡ A Q J
   ◊ A Q
   ♣ K Q J

4. ♠ A K Q 7
   ♡ K Q J 9
   ◊ A K 5 4
   ♣ 3

5. ♠ A 3
   ♡ A Q J 9
   ◊ A K 6
   ♣ A K J 3

YOUR PARTNER HAS OPENED THE AUCTION with two clubs and your partnership has agreed to play double negatives. Your right hand opponent passes. Count your evaluated points. What is your call?

6. ♠ A Q 5 4
   ♡ J 7 3
   ◊ 5 3 2
   ♣ 9 8 4

7. ♠ J 10 9 8 7 6
   ♡ - - - -
   ◊ K J 8 3
   ♣ J 3 2

8. ♠ A 9 3 2
   ♡ K 5
   ◊ 8 7 6 5
   ♣ 8 7 4

9. ♠ 7
   ♡ A Q 9 8 4
   ◊ K J 5 4 3
   ♣ 5 4

10. ♠ Q J 10 9
    ♡ A 9
    ◊ K J 10 9 8 7
    ♣ 2

YOUR PARTNER HAS OPENED THE AUCTION with two clubs and your partnership has agreed to play double negatives. You have correctly responded two diamonds and partner rebids two spades. What is your call?

11. ♠ J 2
    ♡ Q J 5 4
    ◊ Q 10 8 2
    ♣ Q 10 7

12. ♠ 3
    ♡ 8 7 5 3
    ◊ Q 5 3 2
    ♣ 9 8 7 4

13. ♠ J 9 7 4
    ♡ J 5 4 3 2
    ◊ 10 7
    ♣ 9 6

14. ♠ Q 8 4
    ♡ A 5 4 2
    ◊ 3 2
    ♣ J 10 9 7

15. ♠ 3 2
    ♡ A J 9 8 7 5
    ◊ Q 7 2
    ♣ 5 3

YOUR PARTNER HAS OPENED THE AUCTION with two clubs and rebids two no trump over your diamond response. What is your call?

16. ♠ J 7 4 3
    ♡ Q 3 2
    ◊ 5 4 2
    ♣ 10 9 7

17. ♠ J 7 4 3
    ♡ Q 5 3 2
    ◊ 5 4
    ♣ 10 9 7

18. ♠ Q J 10 8 7
    ♡ 5 4
    ◊ Q 5 3 2
    ♣ 7 2

19. ♠ Q 10 9 7 6
    ♡ K 5 4 3 2
    ◊ 3 2
    ♣ 4

20. ♠ Q J 9
    ♡ Q J 10 3
    ◊ Q J 8
    ♣ 7 6 3

21. ♠ 8 5 2
    ♡ J 9 8 7
    ◊ 10 8 3 2
    ♣ 9 4

22. ♠ 3 2
    ♡ J 10 9 7 6 2
    ◊ 8 7 6 4
    ♣ 9

23. ♠ 3
    ♡ A 4
    ◊ 5 4 2
    ♣ Q J 10 9 8 7 6

24. ♠ ----
    ♡ K J 5 4 3 2
    ◊ 10 2
    ♣ K 10 9 8 7

25. ♠ A Q J 10
    ♡ 5 4 3
    ◊ 10 9 8 4
    ♣ 8 7

YOUR PARTNER HAS OPENED THE AUCTION with two clubs. In each case you have made a positive response and your partner has rebid spades. As a double problem, determine (A) your original positive response and (B) your rebid over partner's spade bid.

26. ♠ 3
    ♡ A Q J 5 4
    ◊ Q 10 3 2
    ♣ 7 5 2

27. ♠ Q 10 7
    ♡ J 2
    ◊ A K 10 7
    ♣ J 8 4 2

28. ♠ 3 2
    ♡ A Q J 9
    ◊ Q 10 8 7
    ♣ 9 5 3

29. ♠ K J 3
   ♡ K Q 10
   ◇ K 9 8 7 6 5
   ♣ 8

30. ♠ J 7 2
   ♡ K J 10 2
   ◇ Q J 9 8
   ♣ Q 2

31. ♠ Q 2
   ♡ ----
   ◇ A K Q 10 9 8 7
   ♣ A 5 3 2

YOU ARE LOOKING AT THESE VERY GOOD HANDS. Count your points and (a) determine what to open and (b) if you elect to open a strong two club bid, what is your rebid if partner responds two diamonds?

1.

♠ A Q J 9 7 3
♡ A Q 8
◊ K J 8
♣ 2

ONE SPADE. This doesn't even resemble a two club opening bid. You have a total of 20 points (17 in high cards and 3 for distribution).

2.

♠ A K Q J 7 6 2
♡ A K 2
◊ A 2
♣ 7

TWO CLUBS. This is a solid two club opening bid. Your intention is to rebid spades over your partner's response. You have 26 points (21 in high cards and 5 points in distribution -- 2 points for the singleton, 1 point for the doubleton and 2 points for the spade length).

3.

♠ K J 9 7 3
♡ A Q J
◊ A Q
♣ K Q J

TWO CLUBS. You have 23 high card points and, although you may count an extra point for your doubleton diamond, we recommend a two no trump rebid since the spade suit is rather weak.

4.

♠ A K Q 7
♡ K Q J 9
◊ A K 5 4
♣ 3

ONE DIAMOND. Although you have the necessary points (22 in high cards plus 2 distributional points for the singleton club) for an opening bid of two clubs, it would leave you with no convenient rebid, since you have no five-card suit, and you cannot rebid no trump with a singleton. Hopefully, partner will respond to your one diamond bid, after which you will force the auction to at least game.

5.

♠ A 3
♡ A Q J 9
◊ A K 6
♣ A K J 3

TWO CLUBS. You have 26 high card points and your rebid will be three no trump, showing a balanced 25 to 27 HCP.

YOUR PARTNER HAS OPENED THE AUCTION with two clubs and your partnership has agreed to play double negatives. Your right hand opponent passes. Count your evaluated points. What is your call?

6.

♠ A Q 5 4
♡ J 7 3
◊ 5 3 2
♣ 9 8 4

TWO DIAMONDS. You have 7 high card points, and the possession of two controls (the ace of spades) does not entitle you to add to this. If partner rebids two no trump you will raise him to three. If partner rebids a suit, you will raise him one level to indicate a maximum two diamond bid with a fit.

7.

♠ J 10 9 8 7 6
♡ - - - -
◊ K J 8 3
♣ J 3 2

TWO DIAMONDS. Remember, distributional points do not count until partner has defined his hand. For instance, if partner rebids two hearts, your heart void is a liability; if partner rebids anything else, you may then add three points for your heart void and take an aggressive position.

8.

♠ A 9 3 2
♡ K 5
◊ 8 7 6 5
♣ 8 7 4

TWO NO TRUMP. Although you only have 7 HCP, the possession of three controls allows you to add one point, giving you eight evaluated points, adding up to a minimum positive response.

9.

♠ 7
♡ A Q 9 8 4
◊ K J 5 4 3
♣ 5 4

TWO HEARTS. You have 10 high card points plus one for the three controls (ace of hearts and king of diamonds). You should plan to show your diamond suit on the next round of bidding.

10.

♠ Q J 10 9
♡ A 9
◊ K J 10 9 8 7
♣ 2

THREE DIAMONDS. You should not bid two diamonds, which is the negative response. With your 11 high card points (12 evaluated points) a slam is likely if a fit can be discovered.

YOUR PARTNER HAS OPENED THE AUCTION with two clubs and your partnership has agreed to play double negatives. You have correctly responded two diamonds and partner rebids two spades. What is your call?

11.
♠ J 2
♡ Q J 5 4
◊ Q 10 8 2
♣ Q 10 7

TWO NO TRUMP. Although you have 8 high card points, you had to devalue your hand because of the lack of controls. The two no trump bid tells your partner that you do have some high cards although you have no convenient suit to bid.

12.
♠ 3
♡ 8 7 5 3
◊ Q 5 3 2
♣ 9 8 7 4

THREE CLUBS. This is the second of the double negative bids. It tells partner that you have neither a fit nor a useful bid to make. Partner will now know that you have a near yarborough and will be able to act accordingly.

13.
♠ J 9 7 4
♡ J 5 4 3 2
◊ 10 7
♣ 9 6

FOUR SPADES. Here again you have a very poor hand, but partner has rebid a suit in which you have four card support. You have no desire for partner to proceed past game since you have nothing to show him, so you proceed directly to game.

14.
♠ Q 8 4
♡ A 5 4 2
◊ 3 2
♣ J 10 9 7

THREE SPADES. This tells partner that you have a maximum two diamond response (seven evaluated points) and a fit in the spade suit. If partner decides to explore further, you are willing, since he cannot expect more than you have, after your initial two diamond response.

15.
♠ 3 2
♡ A J 9 8 7 5
◊ Q 7 2
♣ 5 3

THREE HEARTS. Again, you have a maximum two diamond response, but in this case you have a meager fit for partner. If hearts are supported, you should investigate for slam.

YOUR PARTNER HAS OPENED THE AUCTION with two clubs and rebids two no trump over your diamond response. What is your call?

16.
♠ J 7 4 3
♡ Q 3 2
◇ 5 4 2
♣ 10 9 7

THREE NO TRUMP. While you're not in love with this hand, you do have 3 high card points, and partner has promised 23-24. You are therefore in the game range, and are under an obligation to bid game.

17.
♠ J 7 4 3
♡ Q 5 3 2
◇ 5 4
♣ 10 9 7

THREE CLUBS. This is the Stayman convention, which asks partner to bid his four card major if he has one. If partner has a major, you bid game in that suit, since you gain a distributional point for your doubleton diamond. If partner has no four card major, you should bid three no trump.

18.
♠ Q J 10 8 7
♡ 5 4
◇ Q 5 3 2
♣ 7 2

THREE SPADES. This simply requests partner to bid four spades with a spade fit (three or more spades), or to bid three no trump with a doubleton spade. The three spade bid is forcing, but partner should know that you do not have a very good hand, after your original two diamond response.

19.
♠ Q 10 9 7 6
♡ K 5 4 3 2
◇ 3 2
♣ 4

THREE SPADES. As in the last problem, you are asking partner to bid four spades with three or more spades. Here, however, if partner responds three no trump, you will bid four hearts. Partner will then know that you have two five card major suits and act accordingly. If partner bids four spades after the three spade rebid, you might consider bidding again, since your hand re-evaluates to eight points in support of spades (five points in high cards, one for the doubleton diamond and two for the singleton club.) Five hearts would be a slam try and partner, with a good heart fit, might carry on to six spades or six hearts.

20.
♠ Q J 9
♡ Q J 10 3
◊ Q J 8
♣ 7 6 3

FOUR NO TRUMP. You have 9 high card points which you are forced to devalue to 7 evaluated points because you have no controls. When partner rebids no trump, however, you have enough points to wish to be in six no trump if he has a maximum of 24 HCP.

21.
♠ 8 5 2
♡ J 9 8 7
◊ 10 8 3 2
♣ 9 4

PASS. It is, of course, possible that your partner may make three no trump if all the suits break well, and if your one jack is of some great help, but the odds are that partner cannot make game and will probably have trouble in two no trump.

22.
♠ 3 2
♡ J 10 9 7 6 2
◊ 8 7 6 4
♣ 9

THREE HEARTS. If partner bids four hearts you will pass. If partner bids three no trump you bid four hearts to show your six card suit. Although you have only one high card point, you gain four points for distribution (one for the doubleton spade, two for the singleton club, and a point for the heart length). This should give you a chance to make game opposite your partner's strong hand, and four hearts will have more of a chance than three no trump.

23.
♠ 3
♡ A 4
◊ 5 4 2
♣ Q J 10 9 8 7 6

FIVE CLUBS. Partner will know that you have a maximum two diamond bid and a good six or seven card club suit. With a fit and controls, partner should bid a slam in clubs.

24.
♠ ----
♡ K J 5 4 3 2
◊ 10 2
♣ K 10 9 8 7

THREE HEARTS. Although you had to make a negative response on the first round of bidding, the knowledge that your partner does not have a distributional hand, and therefore most probably has a good fit for one of your suits, makes slam a distinct possibility. If partner raises hearts, you might consider jumping to six hearts, while if partner bids three no trump, you should bid four clubs. A good three card holding in either of your suits will be adequate to give you a good play for slam.

25.

♠ A Q J 10
♡ 5 4 3
◊ 10 9 8 4
♣ 8 7

THREE CLUBS. Although you are asking for the majors, you are only interested in the spade suit. If partner responds three spades, you bid four since you gain a point for your doubleton club. If Partner bids anything else, then bid three no trump.

YOUR PARTNER HAS OPENED THE AUCTION with two clubs. In each case you have made a positive response and your partner has rebid spades. As a double problem, determine (A) your original positive response and (B) your rebid over partner's spade bid.

26.

♠ 3
♡ A Q J 5 4
◊ Q 10 3 2
♣ 7 5 2

(A) TWO HEARTS. (B) THREE DIAMONDS. Your original positive response should have been two hearts. Over partner's two spade bid, you should show your second suit by bidding three diamonds. Two no trump would be an error because of your weakness in clubs. If no trump is to be the final contract, your partner should bid it.

27.

♠ Q 10 7
♡ J 2
◊ A K 10 7
♣ J 8 4 2

(A) TWO NO TRUMP. (B) FOUR DIAMONDS. Two no trump was your correct positive response. Over partner's three spade bid, you should now bid four diamonds. Your partner will know that you don't have a long diamond suit since you did not bid three diamonds in response to his original two club bid; he will then be able to figure out that your strength is in diamonds, and that you can support spades. Slam is very likely, and as much information should be exchanged at as low a level as possible. You may even have seven in the hand if partner has good controls!

28.

♠ 3 2
♡ A Q J 9
◊ Q 10 8 7
♣ 9 5 3

(A) TWO NO TRUMP. (B) THREE NO TRUMP. You should have bid two no trump over your partner's two club bid, and when partner bids three spades you should bid three no trump. Your positive response is in the minimum range and you do not have a fit. Any further encouragement should come from partner.

29.

♠ K J 3
♡ K Q 10
◊ K 9 8 7 6 5
♣ 8

(A) THREE DIAMONDS. (B) FOUR NO TRUMP. You should have responded three diamonds to your partner's two club opener. When partner rebids three spades your hand has become very good, and the likelihood of at least a small slam is great. Your next bid is four no trump; if partner has all four aces you should contract for a grand slam in spades. If partner only has three aces, then you must settle for six spades. If partner has only two aces, you should become angry at him for opening a two club bid with such a poor hand.

30.

♠ J 7 2
♡ K J 10 2
◊ Q J 9 8
♣ Q 2

(A) TWO NO TRUMP. (B) FOUR SPADES. Your original positive response should be two no trump, and when partner rebids three spades, you should simply bid four spades. Partner will then know that you have a minimum positive response with a spade fit; any further investigation should come from partner.

31.

♠ Q 2
♡ ----
◊ A K Q 10
    9 8 7
♣ A 5 3 2

(A) THREE DIAMONDS. (B) FOUR NO TRUMP. You were quite happy to hear partner open with a strong two club bid, and your correct response was, of course, three diamonds. When partner rebids three spades, you should rebid four no trump. If partner has two aces, bid seven no trump; if partner has only one ace, you should be mildly surprised -- but bid seven spades anyway! If partner is missing the ace of hearts his spade suit must be excellent, a minimum of A K J 10 9 6 4, and your diamond suit should run.

Chapter 4

DEFENSE
AGAINST THE WEAK TWO BID

4

TO THE EXTENT YOU HAVE UNDERSTOOD the first three chapters, you now know the theory of the weak two and the strong, forcing two club opening bid. This is where most text books would stop, but in fact this is where we must begin, since to use the weak two bid effectively, one must not only understand the bid itself, but also how to defend against it. This is not as straightforward as it may seem, since not only may the opener preempt, but the responder may elect to make psychic responses to further confound your bidding problems. We will now discuss both the proper defensive procedures after a weak two bid and also after some unexpected responses that may occur at the table.

BIDDING OVER AN OPPOSING WEAK TWO BID

A. DIRECT POSITION

For our purposes there are three types of hands to be considered:
(a). Less than twelve points -- A hand with which we did not intend
      to open the bidding under any condition.
(b). The minimum opening bid -- Twelve to fifteen high card points.
(c). The better than minimum opening bid -- Sixteen high card
      points or better.
It is obvious that hands of type (a) do not come into consideration when our right hand opponent opens a weak two bid. We simply pass, as we intended to do in any event. Whether or not we take action on a hand of type (b) depends entirely upon our distribution. On hand (c) we must take some action; the type of action we take is dependent both on our high card count and on our distribution. The general approach to a decision whether or not to take any action on the (b) hand over an opponent's weak two bid is basically the same as the decision whether to take action over an opponent's opening one bid -- the only difference is in the factor of safety because the

71

auction after the weak two bid begins one level higher. For example, assume that your right hand opponent has opened with a weak two spade bid. Consider the following five hands:

(1) ♠ A Q x x
     ♡ x x
     ◇ K J x x
     ♣ K x x

(2) ♠ x x x
     ♡ A J
     ◇ K Q 10 x x
     ♣ K J x

(3) ♠ K x
     ♡ A Q x x
     ◇ K x x x
     ♣ Q J x

(4) ♠ x x
     ♡ K J x x
     ◇ K Q x x
     ♣ A 10 x

(5) ♠ K Q J x
     ♡ A x x
     ◇ A x x
     ♣ J x x

On the first hand you should pass, just as you would had your opponent opened one spade. You have insufficient high card points for a no trump overcall and a take out double would misrepresent your hand. On the second hand you must also pass. The preempt is annoying since, with no opposing bidding, you would have opened the auction with one diamond. You cannot afford to make a take out double, because your partner might bid the heart suit at the three level, and your diamond suit is too broken to overcall with safely. The third hand is a different story. Here a take out double would be in order. Your king of spades is a very good card with a weak two spade bid at your right and you have admirable support for the other suits, especially the heart suit. Hand (4) is an illustration of the safety factor that must be taken into account. If your right hand opponent had opened the bidding one spade, a take out double would be acceptable. However, since he has opened with a weak two bid the double is very dangerous, and we would pass. Partner would need quite a good hand to reach a safe contract. If the high card strength lies with your left hand opponent rather than your partner, you might land in serious trouble by entering the auction. On hand (5) you should clearly pass, much as you did on the first hand. So far, the opponents have bid your best suit, and if they bid further you may be able to exact a good penalty. You are a trifle too weak to bid no trump freely at the two level, so you should not enter the auction.

Hand type (c) is the "big hand" and will be discussed in the next section, since it is handled in almost the same way whether you are in direct position or fourth (balancing) position.

B. BALANCING (FOURTH) POSITION

Here, as in the direct position, we must consider three different hand types. The difference is that we may take action on some hands of type (a) (less than twelve points) since partner may have been unable to make a bid with a big hand because he was shut out by the preempt. The problems in the balancing seat are further complicated by the fact that the partner of the weak two bidder may have made a bid. We will therefore consider two different problems:

(1) When third hand has passed his partner's weak two bid;

(2) When third hand has acted over his partner's weak two bid.

Let us consider the simplest case first, when the opponent and your partner have both passed the weak two bid. Assume that your left hand opponent has opened the bidding with a weak two heart bid. Your partner has passed, and your right hand opponent has passed. Consider each of the following five hands:

(1) ♠ K Q 10 x	(2) ♠ A K x x	(3) ♠ K J 9 8
♡ A x	♡ x	♡ K J 10 9
◊ K 10 x x	◊ K x x x	◊ Q J x x
♣ x x x	♣ J x x x	♣ Q

(4) ♠ x x	(5) ♠ Q J 10 x x
♡ A J x	♡ A Q
◊ J 9 8 7 5	◊ Q J x x x
♣ A K x	♣ x

The first hand is a minimum type (b) hand and with good support for the unbid major, a take out double would be in order. Partner is marked with a certain number of high cards and may have been trapped and unable to bid due to his distribution. The second hand, type (a), would be passed in direct position, but in balancing seat the take out double is clearly in order. Partner may have quite a good hand but his heart holding may be such that he was unable to act over the weak two bid. You have fine support for any suit he might elect to bid, and passing out the weak two bid would give too much credit to its preemptive value.

Although hand three is a type (b) hand of opening bid strength, you must consider the following facts: Partner is marked by the bidding with a shortage in hearts, yet he failed to take any action over the opponent's weak two heart bid. This should indicate that his hand is not very good. We therefore recommend a pass with this hand as the best way to avoid trouble and attain a possible plus score. Hand four should also be passed, despite the fact that it is a type (b) hand. We cannot make a take out double because of our weak spade holding, and an overcall in the diamond suit would be much too dangerous. On hand five the balancer should bid two spades in preference to a take out double, for two reasons. Firstly, he cannot support the club suit if partner should elect to bid clubs, and if he doubles and then bids either diamonds or spades over partner's three club bid, he would be describing a stronger hand than he actually has. Secondly, he would prefer the lead to come up to the ace-queen of hearts rather than through them, consequently he should strive to become declarer. If partner bids three clubs over the two spade bid, he can then bid three diamonds, effectively describing a two suiter.

More complicated is the case where the partner of the weak two bidder elects to respond either preemptively or with a forcing action. One very good rule to remember is that when the opponents are in the middle of a forcing sequence, stay out of the bidding. They may get themselves into trouble. If you have a very fine hand, your partner is probably marked with a yarborough.

When you have been "preempted against," it is more difficult and you should enter the auction only with either a type (c) hand that contains appropriate distribution or with a hand containing a suit that offers some degree of safety. In the light of this, consider the following situations:

You are in balancing (fourth) position, and your left hand opponent has opened the bidding with two hearts. Your partner has passed, and your right hand opponent has bid four hearts. What call do you make with each of the following five hands?

(1) ♠ A Q x x x
     ♡ ----
     ◊ A K x x
     ♣ Q 10 x x

(2) ♠ A K Q J 9 8 7
     ♡ A 5
     ◊ 3
     ♣ A Q 3

(3) ♠ Q J 9
     ♡ Q J 3
     ◊ Q J 10 3
     ♣ A K 7

(4) ♠ Q J 10 9 8
     ♡ A
     ◊ K Q J 9 8 7
     ♣ 2

(5) ♠ x
     ♡ A J 10
     ◊ A K Q J 5 2
     ♣ K J 10

On the first hand you should make a take out double. Although it is somewhat risky, it seems evident that the opponents are out to steal the contract and your support for all three suits should

74

provide a reasonable margin of safety. On hand one, we suspected the opponents might be "stealing" -- on hand two, with our twenty count and solid spade suit, we know that they are. We believe that a four spade bid in this seat would be "lazy" and recommend instead a leap to five spades. Partner should realize that we have a huge hand with a completely self sufficient spade suit, and should carry on to six with very little. There is, of course, some risk that we may end up in five spades going down one, but then, bridge is a risky game.

On hand three we must pass with our sixteen points. We have been properly "fixed" by the preempt, and must simply hope to beat four hearts. On hand four a problem is presented, since we don't really know if the hand belongs in spades or diamonds. An acceptable action would be to double; if partner bids five clubs, we will bid five diamonds. Partner should know that we are two-suited with diamonds and spades, and should also know that our hand is not necessarily as big as it sounds, because we have been trapped by the preempt. If this last concept is too ambiguous for your partnership, then an alternate call would be four no trump (which requests partner to bid his better minor); again if partner bids five clubs we bid five diamonds showing a two suiter in diamonds and spades.

On hand five we should bid five diamonds, undeterred by the four heart bid. Partner should have a singleton heart, and even if he does have a yarborough, we should not be hurt too badly. We would expect to be down one, losing two clubs and a spade. Partner may have quite a fine hand, in which case we have missed a slam. But again, we have been preempted against, and must struggle to find the proper contract.

We mentioned you should not enter the auction if the opponents are in the midst of a forcing sequence. This rule should be tempered with judgment, of course. For instance, if it appears obvious to you that the opponents are trying to steal the contract, then it pays to enter the bidding before it gets out of hand. Another point is that a forcing auction may quickly become a non-forcing auction:

South	West	North	East
2♠	Pass	2NT	Pass
3♡	Pass	3♠	?

North's last bid is non-forcing; in fact it requests South to pass. Something is wrong; if North was investigating for game, and South says he has a good hand, it is unusual for North to wish to close out the bidding. To prepare yourself for this sort of sequence, assume that your left hand opponent has opened the bidding with two hearts, your partner passes, and your right hand opponent bids two no trump (Ogust). What action should you take on each of the following hands?

(1)	♠ A K J 10 x x	(2)	♠ x x	(3)	♠ A J x x
	♡ A J x		♡ A		♡ Q 10 9 8
	◊ K J x		◊ A K Q J 10 9 8		◊ Q J x
	♣ x		♣ Q 10 2		♣ A Q

On hand one, you should pass. This may seem surprising, but think a moment. The weak two bidder is forced to respond over the two no trump bid. For you to bid at this moment would clarify the situation for your opponents. Your spade suit is good enough that you can enter the auction later, and you may find out some interesting things about the hand in the meantime.

On hand two, you should bid three no trump. The hand may very well belong to the opponents, because of your lack of major suit protection. The three no trump bid serves as a preemptive action against the spade suit that might be held by your right hand opponent. If either opponent bids four hearts, you might even consider bidding four no trump; if partner bids four spades, you should be pleased, since partner knows you don't have good spades or else you would have made a take out double, and your singleton ace of hearts combined with the doubleton trump is a definite asset.

On hand three you should pass. You have a solid one no trump opener, but the opponents are on their way to trouble. If they reach game you can certainly double it. Your ace-queen of clubs are likely to be favorably placed, because the odds are that the weak two bidder does not have the king.

In the discussion of the preceding hands we have carefully avoided stating the vulnerability. Needless to say, the risk factor is greatly increased if we are vulnerable against non-vulnerable opponents, and reduced if the vulnerability is favorable. With a hand that is "marginal," whether you elect to bid or pass is affected by the vulnerability, and your decision should primarily be based on the risk involved.

The type (c) hand (better than a minimum opening bid) is the easiest type with which to enter the bidding after an opposing weak two bid. Here we have more than a minimum opening bid; so long as we keep the safety factor in mind, there should be no problem.

There are three basic ways to enter the auction after an opposing weak two bid:

1. A no trump overcall.
2. A take out double.
3. An overcall in a suit.

The first two are easily defined and primarily have the same requirements whether in direct position or in balancing position.

1. The no trump overcall. To overcall an opposing weak two bid with two no trump, we should have between a good sixteen and a poor nineteen high card points. With less than sixteen you should pass; with more than nineteen you should double and then rebid no trump. Notice that the no trump range is about a point higher than we would normally use to open the bidding with one no trump, to include the safety factor that is necessary when acting over an opposing weak two bid. In addition, the suit that we are overcalling should be at least doubly stopped since we can be reasonably sure that it will be the opening lead. In deciding whether or not you have the type of hand with which to overcall two no trump, keep in mind that partner will raise to three no trump with eight high card points.

2. The take out double. While the distribution does not have to be quite as perfect as it must be with a hand of minimum strength there is every chance that partner will respond on the three level; therefore you should be able to support any suit he bids, unless your hand is so strong that you can bid your own suit over his response. Your take out double suggests shortness in the weak two bidder's suit, but should have enough quick tricks to be able to stand a penalty pass by partner, in case he decides to pass out your double.

3. The overcall of a suit. In direct position it is quite acceptable to make a simple overcall in a suit, even if you have an excellent hand. In balancing position you should be wary of not describing your values sufficiently. As an example, assume that the opponents have opened the auction with two hearts, and you have the following:

♠ A K J 9 x x   ♡ A x   ♢ K Q x   ♣ x x

In direct position, a two spade bid would be acceptable since you imply a reasonably good hand by acting directly over the opponent's weak bid. In balancing position the proper bid is a double followed by a spade bid, since you would overcall two spades in balancing position with a hand as weak as:

♠ A J 10 x x   ♥ K x   ♦ A x x   ♣ x x x

Assume that your right hand opponent has opened the bidding with two hearts. What call would make you on each of the following excellent hands?

(1) ♠ A Q x x	(2) ♠ Q x	(3) ♠ A K Q 10 x x
♥ x	♥ A Q x	♥ x
♦ A Q x x	♦ K J x x	♦ x
♣ K J x x	♣ A K 10 x	♣ A Q 10 x x

(4) ♠ K Q x	(5) ♠ A Q
♥ K 10 x	♥ A K 10
♦ A Q x x	♦ A K 8 x
♣ Q x x	♣ J 9 x x

On the first hand a take out double is clear cut and excellent. You have sixteen high card points, shortness in opponent's suit and excellent support for the other three suits. If partner responds with two spades you should raise to three spades. The second hand meets the requirements for a two no trump overcall. You have nineteen high card points and a double stopper in the opponent's suit. You would rather have a stronger spade stopper, but unfortunately this is all that was dealt to you.

The third hand is aggressively excellent and you can support two suits admirably. You should therefore make a take out double and, if partner responds with diamonds, you should bid spades. Partner should then be able to figure out that you have a "black" hand with good club and spade support, and should act accordingly. A direct two spade overcall would be a mistake, because any fit with partner should give you a good play for game. It would be acceptable to overcall two spades and bid clubs later, if the opponents were nice and cooperative. Unfortunately, this is not always the case, and they will probably preempt against you in the red suits. You should get more "mileage" from the double.

Hand four is a good example of the weak two bid in action. You have sixteen high card points, but you do not have the opponent's suit doubly stopped. You must therefore pass, and await developments, since it would be much too dangerous to enter the auction with such a marginal hand. For example, suppose you overcall two no trump and your left hand opponent doubles -- you're in a lot of trouble with no place to go.

Hand five is an excellent hand, and a direct two no trump overcall would be a distinct underbid. On this type of hand a double is correct and, over partner's response, you rebid no trump. This shows better than nineteen points with no trump distribution.

* * * *

We will forego the quiz for Chapter Four and will, instead, include some examples of how the great and near-great players have handled the weak two bid, both as an aggressive and as a defensive weapon, and how they have been alternately successful with the weak two bid and confounded by it. Examine the problems of each of the players, and it should become evident why the weak two bid has become one of the most popular tools in bridge.

Dealer: North
Vul: N-S

```
                        ♠ 5 3
                        ♡ 9 4 3
                        ◊ 7 4 2
                        ♣ 9 8 6 4 2
      ♠ Q J 10 9 2                      ♠ 4
      ♡ 5                N              ♡ A K 10 8 7 6
      ◊ A K J 3      W       E          ◊ 9 8 5
      ♣ K J 5            S              ♣ 10 7 3
                        ♠ A K 8 7 6
                        ♡ Q J 2
                        ◊ Q 10 6
                        ♣ A Q
```

South	West	North	East
---	---	Pass	2♡
2NT	Dbl.	3♣	Pass
Pass	Dbl.	Pass	Pass
Pass			

THIS HAND IS A CLASSIC EXAMPLE of the pitfalls presented to the opponents of the weak two bidder. Certainly, no one can blame South for entering the auction after East's non-vulnerable two heart opening. (Whether he bids two no trump or two spades or doubles does not change the end result greatly.) The result of the two no trump overcall was catastrophic. West doubled and North-South had no good place to run to. They ended up in three clubs doubled and the defense was fairly automatic. East took his ace and king of hearts, and then led a third heart for his partner to ruff. West cashed the king of diamonds and switched to the queen of spades. North won the trick in dummy, and played the ace and queen of clubs. West won the king and returned a second spade for East to ruff. Two more diamond tricks resulted in eight tricks for the defense, down 1100 points. It is doubtful that the result would have been so calamitous had not East-West been playing weak two bids.

North-South —1100

Dealer: East
Vul: Both

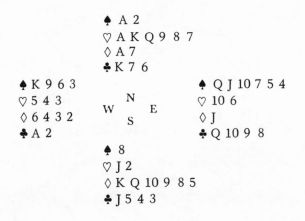

♠ A 2
♡ A K Q 9 8 7
◇ A 7
♣ K 7 6

♠ K 9 6 3   ♠ Q J 10 7 5 4
♡ 5 4 3   N   ♡ 10 6
◇ 6 4 3 2   W   E   ◇ J
♣ A 2   S   ♣ Q 10 9 8

♠ 8
♡ J 2
◇ K Q 10 9 8 5
♣ J 5 4 3

South	West	North	East
---	---	---	2♠
Pass	4♠	5♡	Pass
Pass	Pass		

A COMMON ADVANTAGE gained by the weak two bid is the "continued preemption" when the partner of the opening weak two bidder can raise or jump raise opener's suit, further confounding the opponent's communications. In this hand, South has no convenient action over East's initial two spade bid, and West's four spade bid makes it practically impossible for North-South to arrive at their cold slam. As a matter of fact, North's five heart bid was dangerous as it was, since there was no guarantee that it would make. And South cannot be blamed for passing with his meager holdings, for North could have much less for his bid. There is no doubt that, left to their own devices, North-South would have reached one of their slams.

North-South + 710

Dealer: South
Vul: East-West

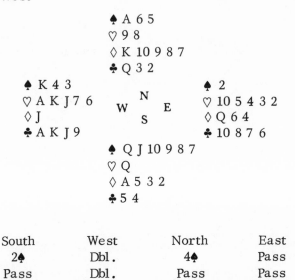

```
                    ♠ A 6 5
                    ♡ 9 8
                    ◊ K 10 9 8 7
                    ♣ Q 3 2
    ♠ K 4 3                        ♠ 2
    ♡ A K J 7 6      N             ♡ 10 5 4 3 2
    ◊ J           W     E          ◊ Q 6 4
    ♣ A K J 9        S             ♣ 10 8 7 6
                    ♠ Q J 10 9 8 7
                    ♡ Q
                    ◊ A 5 3 2
                    ♣ 5 4
```

South	West	North	East
2♠	Dbl.	4♠	Pass
Pass	Dbl.	Pass	Pass
Pass			

WEST HAD NO PROBLEM finding a take out double with his type (c) hand after South's weak two spade opening. North applied the principle of "continued preemption" and bid four spades. When that bid came around to East, he doubled again, and the final contract became four spades doubled. West led the king of hearts, and then continued with the ace, which South ruffed. He then finessed the king of spades, pulled trump and, when the jack of diamonds fell under the king, he applied the principle of "restricted choice" and finessed East for the queen. On the fifth diamond he discarded a club. Conceding a club, he claimed four spades doubled with an overtrick. As mentioned earlier, one of the most delightful surprises of a continued preemption is that occasionally partner will make his contract. Note also that East-West are cold for four hearts, and five is dependent only on the location of the queen of clubs. Due to the preemptive bidding, however, it was very difficult for East-West to enter the bidding on the five level.

North-South   690

Dealer: South
Vul: Both

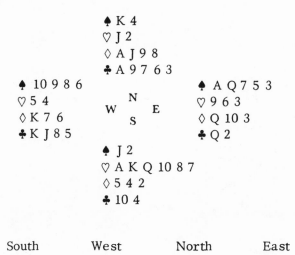

♠ K 4
♡ J 2
◇ A J 9 8
♣ A 9 7 6 3

♠ 10 9 8 6
♡ 5 4
◇ K 7 6
♣ K J 8 5

N
W   E
S

♠ A Q 7 5 3
♡ 9 6 3
◇ Q 10 3
♣ Q 2

♠ J 2
♡ A K Q 10 8 7
◇ 5 4 2
♣ 10 4

South	West	North	East
2♡	Pass	2NT (Ogust)	Pass
3NT	Pass	Pass	Pass

A SKILLFUL USE OF ANY BIDDING CONVENTION involves giving your partner all of the necessary information to determine the final contract, while giving a minimum of information to the opponents. Here, South was happy to bid three no trump over his partner's two no trump (Ogust) bid, since he has a solid six card heart suit. Now, East has to lead against three no trump. An opening spade lead results in giving North an immediate nine tricks with six hearts, the king of spades and two minor suit aces. As it turns out, if East leads anything except the spade, North would not have made his contract, since West would have been on lead sooner or later to lead through the doubleton king of spades. Can you blame East for leading a spade? Not many people would. Nevertheless, this is part of the problem in making decisions against an auction in which the only people who know what is going on are the opponents.   North-South + 600

Dealer: South
Vul: Both

```
                    ♠ A K 10 9 7
                    ♡ K J 9 7
                    ◊ 6
                    ♣ 8 7 3
  ♠ Q J 8 6            N          ♠ 5 4 2
  ♡ 8 6 5          W      E       ♡ 4 3
  ◊ K J 8             S          ◊ 5 4 2
  ♣ Q J 10                        ♣ A K 9 6 4
                    ♠ 3
                    ♡ A Q 10 2
                    ◊ A Q 10 9 7 3
                    ♣ 5 3
```

South	West	North	East
2◊ !	Pass	2♠	Pass
3◊	Pass	Pass	Pass

THE CORRECT USE OF THE WEAK TWO BID often produces results that are not attainable in any other way. By contrast, incorrect use of the bid can also produce results not as desirable, that are not obtainable in any other way. South's opening weak two diamond bid is sadly incorrect. First, the hand is simply too strong for a weak two bid. Second, and even more important, he has a four card major. North took aggressive action by bidding two spades (it would not have been incorrect to pass), and South could have saved the hand by bidding two no trump, allowing North to bid three hearts. After the actual three diamond rebid, North passed, convinced that there was no future in the hand. South succeeded in making three diamonds (losing two clubs and two diamonds), but it is evident that four hearts can be made. South should open one diamond and permit North to show the major suits.

North-South + 110

Dealer: North
Vul: Both

```
                    ♠ 7 3
                    ♡ K 7 6 2
                    ◊ 10 8 6 4
                    ♣ Q 10 9
      ♠ J 9 8              N         ♠ 6 5 4
      ♡ Q J 10       W         E     ♡ A 9 8
      ◊ K J                S         ◊ A Q 3 2
      ♣ A K 8 7 6                    ♣ 5 3 2
                    ♠ A K Q 10 2
                    ♡ 5 4 3
                    ◊ 9 7 5
                    ♣ J 4
```

South	West	North	East
---	---	Pass	Pass
2♠	Pass!	Pass	Pass

AFTER SOUTH'S THIRD HAND WEAK TWO SPADE BID, West deserves praise for his disciplined pass. Indeed, the pass is 100% correct, since he does not have 16 points which would justify unilateral action, and his distribution does not justify a take out double. North passed, and East did not have enough to re-open the bidding. The defense was excellent. West led the queen of hearts, which held the trick. He continued with the jack of hearts, which was also allowed to hold, then led a third heart to East's ace. East switched to a low diamond, won by West's jack. West then cashed the ace and king of clubs and followed with the king of diamonds. East overtook with the ace, played the queen of diamonds and then, to add icing to the cake, returned the last diamond to promote the jack of trumps in West's hand. Final result: North-South down four for -400. Indeed, this may have been the best result available for North-South, since East-West can bid and make three no trump against any defense except a spade opening lead. We cannot argue with South's third hand two spade bid, since it serves as a lead director in case West bids. There was certainly no indication that South would go down four; East-West would have doubled if they had any inkling of the final result. North-South —400

85

Dealer: South
Vul: East-West

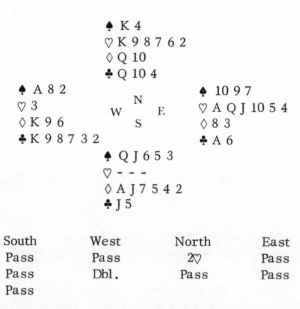

```
                    ♠ K 4
                    ♡ K 9 8 7 6 2
                    ◊ Q 10
                    ♣ Q 10 4
        ♠ A 8 2            N            ♠ 10 9 7
        ♡ 3          W         E        ♡ A Q J 10 5 4
        ◊ K 9 6           S            ◊ 8 3
        ♣ K 9 8 7 3 2                  ♣ A 6
                    ♠ Q J 6 5 3
                    ♡ - - -
                    ◊ A J 7 5 4 2
                    ♣ J 5
```

South	West	North	East
Pass	Pass	2♡	Pass
Pass	Dbl.	Pass	Pass
Pass			

AS WE HAVE MENTIONED MANY TIMES, the weak two bid is a powerful weapon, but the misuse of a powerful weapon can backfire. North's opening 2♡ bid violated one of the basic principles in that the suit should contain two out of the top five honors and should have good texture. While we readily admit that East's heart holding was unusual, North's weak two bid misdescribed the hand to the extent that South did not bid either spades or diamonds after the double was passed by East. As the play went, North was only able to negotiate four tricks and went down four tricks doubled. Either two spades and three diamonds could be made with careful play. While we believe that South should not have passed two hearts doubled, the basic error was by North.

East-West + 700

Dealer: North
Vul: East-West

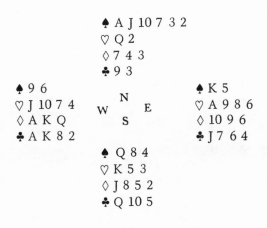

```
                      ♠ A J 10 7 3 2
                      ♡ Q 2
                      ◊ 7 4 3
                      ♣ 9 3
     ♠ 9 6                              ♠ K 5
     ♡ J 10 7 4      N                  ♡ A 9 8 6
     ◊ A K Q       W   E                ◊ 10 9 6
     ♣ A K 8 2       S                  ♣ J 7 6 4
                      ♠ Q 8 4
                      ♡ K 5 3
                      ◊ J 8 5 2
                      ♣ Q 10 5
```

South	West	North	East
---	---	2♠	Pass
3♠	Dbl.	Pass	4♡
4♠	Dbl.	Pass	Pass
Pass			

THIS DEAL RESULTED in a kind of a stand-off. North played 4♠ doubled and went down four tricks. While South might be criticized for his 4♠ bid, it really didn't matter very much since East-West were cold for 620 in 4♡--net loss 80 points. The North and South hands were badly duplicated: hence the down four result. If North could have escaped with down three, he would have gained 120 points, and if North's distribution was happier, he might have escaped for down two which would have been a gain of 320 points. In a sense, South had everything to gain and very little to lose by his four spade bid since North could have had a much better hand.

East-West + 700

Dealer: North
Vul: Both

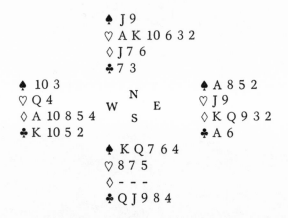

♠ J 9
♡ A K 10 6 3 2
◊ J 7 6
♣ 7 3

♠ 10 3
♡ Q 4
◊ A 10 8 5 4
♣ K 10 5 2

N
W   E
S

♠ A 8 5 2
♡ J 9
◊ K Q 9 3 2
♣ A 6

♠ K Q 7 6 4
♡ 8 7 5
◊ - - -
♣ Q J 9 8 4

South	West	North	East
---	---	2♡	Dbl.
3♡	4◊	Pass	5◊
Pass	Pass	Pass	

SOUTH'S 3♡ BID over East's take out double was designed to cut the East-West communications. When West correctly bid 4◊, East had a problem whether or not to bid 5◊. In this case he bid 5◊ which was set one trick, as West had to lose two heart tricks and one spade. Please notice that the North-South 3♡ contract would not be in severe trouble, and would probably make against any normal defense. The important point of this hand is that East had to make the decision whether or not to bid a game. In this case he made the wrong decision, since the communications were effectively cut by the weak two bid and no form of exploration was possible.

North-South +100

Dealer: North
Vul: Neither

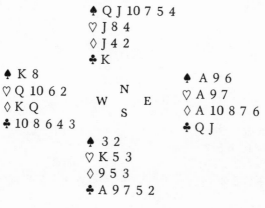

                    ♠ Q J 10 7 5 4
                    ♡ J 8 4
                    ◇ J 4 2
                    ♣ K
    ♠ K 8   ♠ A 9 6
    ♡ Q 10 6 2   N   ♡ A 9 7
    ◇ K Q   W   E   ◇ A 10 8 7 6
    ♣ 10 8 6 4 3   S   ♣ Q J
                    ♠ 3 2
                    ♡ K 5 3
                    ◇ 9 5 3
                    ♣ A 9 7 5 2

South	West	North	East
---	---	2♠	Dbl.
Pass	4♡	Pass	Pass
Pass			

AFTER EAST DOUBLED North's opening weak two bid, West had
a real problem with his ten HCP. His chosen bid of 4♡ turned out
all right since both red suits broke 3-3 and the heart honors were
favorably placed. This did not necessarily have to be the case,
however. With all four hands exposed, the best game contract for
East-West would be 3NT, but West did not have the opportunity to
look at all four hands; he had to make a decision then and there.
For example, if the hearts are 4-2 and the honors are placed properly nine tricks certainly become much easier than ten tricks.
Secondly, if North remains silent in first position, East will probably open with 1NT and over West's two club Stayman bid it would
be much too dangerous for North to enter the bidding with two spades.
This weak two bid interfered with the opponents' communication
with a minimum amount of risk. The opponents solved their problem, but they may not have.   East-West + 420

Dealer: West
Vul: East-West

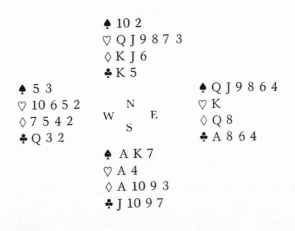

```
                    ♠ 10 2
                    ♡ Q J 9 8 7 3
                    ◇ K J 6
                    ♣ K 5
    ♠ 5 3                         ♠ Q J 9 8 6 4
    ♡ 10 6 5 2         N          ♡ K
    ◇ 7 5 4 2       W     E       ◇ Q 8
    ♣ Q 3 2            S          ♣ A 8 6 4
                    ♠ A K 7
                    ♡ A 4
                    ◇ A 10 9 3
                    ♣ J 10 9 7
```

South	West	North	East
---	Pass	2♡	2♠
4♡	Pass	Pass	Pass

AS IT TURNED OUT, West had no problem over South's four hearts
bid since he did have a yarborough. The key point to notice is that
whether or not you are playing a weak two bid it will be easy enough
to reach a game level contract whether it be in hearts or no trump.
The weak two bid does not conflict in any way with standard bidding
methods, and you will never miss a contract because you are playing weak two bids. The weak two bid poses problems to the opposition; not to your partnership.   North-South +480

Dealer: East
Vul: Both

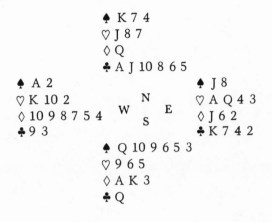

	♠ K 7 4		
	♡ J 8 7		
	◊ Q		
	♣ A J 10 8 6 5		
♠ A 2			♠ J 8
♡ K 10 2	N		♡ A Q 4 3
◊ 10 9 8 7 5 4	W E		◊ J 6 2
♣ 9 3	S		♣ K 7 4 2
	♠ Q 10 9 6 5 3		
	♡ 9 6 5		
	◊ A K 3		
	♣ Q		

South	West	North	East
---	---	---	Pass
2♠	Pass	3♠	Pass
4♠	Pass	Pass	Pass

THIS NORTH-SOUTH PARTNERSHIP play a peculiar variant of the weak two bid in which North's 3♠ bid is invitational to game. When this hand was played by another team, a more exploratory auction was employed which pin-pointed the heart weakness. West duly led the deuce of hearts and the defense took their four top tricks. Faced with a blind auction, West led the nine of clubs and declarer had time to jettison his losing hearts on the ace-king of diamonds. This illustrates another advantage of the weak two bid; it tends to give a minimum of defensive information to the opponents.

North-South + 620

Dealer: South
Vul: East-West

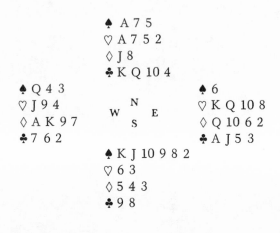

♠ A 7 5
♡ A 7 5 2
◊ J 8
♣ K Q 10 4

♠ Q 4 3
♡ J 9 4
◊ A K 9 7
♣ 7 6 2

♠ 6
♡ K Q 10 8
◊ Q 10 6 2
♣ A J 5 3

♠ K J 10 9 8 2
♡ 6 3
◊ 5 4 3
♣ 9 8

South	West	North	East
2♠	Pass	2NT	Pass
3♣	Pass	3♠	Pass
Pass	Pass		

THE FAVORABLE VULNERABILITY plus the weakness of the hand induced South to employ his "poetic license" and open a weak two bid with only four points and no high card strength outside of his suit. This should never be done opposite an unpassed partner, as is shown by the above deal. North quite correctly bid 2NT to ascertain the strength of partner's hand. Playing Ogust, the 3♣ bid showed no interest and North duly stopped short of game. As the play went, South lost five tricks for down one. As an interesting feature, notice what would have happened if we remove the king of clubs from North's hand and give it to West in place of a low heart. North might employ the same auction and steal the hand from an East-West team which has a good play for five of either minor. The weak two bid has the habit of posing insoluble problems to the defense.

East-West + 50

Dealer: East
Vul: East-West

```
                    ♠ A Q J 10
                    ♡ 6 2
                    ◊ Q J 9 7
                    ♣ Q 7 6
      ♠ 7 6 3                        ♠ K 9 5
      ♡ K 4            N             ♡ Q 9 5 3
      ◊ A 10 6 4 3 2  W   E          ◊ K 8
      ♣ A 3            S             ♣ J 10 8 2
                    ♠ 8 4 2
                    ♡ A J 10 8 7
                    ◊ 5
                    ♣ K 9 5 4
```

South	West	North	East
---	---	---	Pass
Pass	2◊	Pass	Pass
2♡	Pass	2NT	Pass
3♣	Pass	3NT	Dbl.
Pass	Pass	Pass	

SOUTH'S BALANCING BID of 2♡ was correct since North might have
quite a good hand and be unable to enter the auction over the weak
two diamond opener. When North bid 2NT, it is possible that South
should have subsided and prayed for a decent result. However, he
unwisely tried to find a better spot for the hand and North eventual-
ly ended up in 3NT doubled going down three for five hundred points.
Notice how East sat very quietly with an almost absolute knowledge
that North-South would get into trouble, and could certainly not make
a game contract. This is an example of what we stated at the beginning of the book: North-South are confronted with a terribly difficult bidding problem. If they solve their problem, they achieve an
average result. If they do not solve it, catastrophe strikes, as it
did in this hand. In an abstract sense, it was almost automatic for
N-S to be penalized heavily after West opened with a weak two diamond bid. The problems were just too great.   East-West + 500

Dealer: North
Vul: North-South

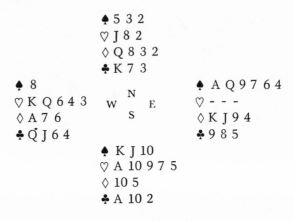

♠ 5 3 2
♡ J 8 2
◊ Q 8 3 2
♣ K 7 3

♠ 8
♡ K Q 6 4 3
◊ A 7 6
♣ Q J 6 4

♠ A Q 9 7 6 4
♡ - - -
◊ K J 9 4
♣ 9 8 5

♠ K J 10
♡ A 10 9 7 5
◊ 10 5
♣ A 10 2

South	West	North	East
---	---	Pass	2♠
Pass	Pass	Pass	

ALTHOUGH EAST'S WEAK TWO SPADE BID turned out to produce a normal partial, we heartily disapprove of the action due to the heart void. West's hand could have been slightly different, in which case two spades would result in a major loss. As an example, change West's hand slightly to the following:

♠ 8   ♡ Q 10 3 2   ◊ A Q 10 8 7   ♣ A 3 2

With the same strength (12 HCPs) West would still pass partner's weak two spade opening and the hand would be a lay down for five diamonds and possibly make six or seven, because the spade suit sets up. Similarly, West could have a hand something like:

♠ - - -   ♡ K 7 4   ◊ Q 6   ♣ A K 8 6 5 4 3

in which case six clubs would be very likely to make, but the hand would play in two spades. The rule of not opening a weak two bid with a void, especially opposite an unpassed partner, should not be forgotten; otherwise you will lose much of the bid's accuracy.

East-West +140

Dealer: East
Vul: East-West

```
                      ♠ A 4 3
                      ♡ 8 5 3
                      ◇ J 8 6 3
                      ♣ 8 6 4
      ♠ K 10 9 6              ♠ Q J 8 7 5 2
      ♡ Q 10 9       N        ♡ K 2
      ◇ A         W     E     ◇ 7 4
      ♣ A Q 5 3 2     S        ♣ K 10 9
                      ♠ - - -
                      ♡ A J 7 6 4
                      ◇ K Q 10 9 5 2
                      ♣ J 7
```

South	West	North	East
- - -	- - -	- - -	2♠
3♡	4♡	Pass	4♠
5◇	5♠	6◇	Pass
Pass	Dbl.	Pass	Pass
Pass			

THIS IS A GOOD EXAMPLE of the accuracy gained with the weak two bid. At the vulnerability, West had little difficulty judging the resources of the combined partnership. If East's spade suit was solid and he did not have an outside king, a five level contract might hinge on a simple club finesse, while if, as in this case, East's spade suit was missing the ace, then he was a moral certainty to have two outside kings for his vulnerable weak two bid. If there were no duplications in diamonds, that is, if East did not have the king of diamonds, then five spades would be a virtual lay down, while if East did have the king of diamonds and the king of hearts, the contract would be likely to depend on a club finesse. The only "disaster situation" would be if East had the king of diamonds and the king of clubs, and was off the ace of spades and two heart tricks. With this in mind, West was able to bid the maximum number of spades that his side could make and finally double the diamond sacrifice at the six level. Please notice that by a similar process of "placing cards" in partner's hand, West could determine that it was highly unlikely that his partner could make a spade slam.

East-West +500

Dealer: South
Vul: North-South

```
                        ♠ - - -
                        ♡ K Q 9 7 2
                        ◇ A K 10 4 3 2
                        ♣ A 3
    ♠ A Q J 10 9 8              N          ♠ K 6 4 3
    ♡ 8                   W          E     ♡ 5
    ◇ Q 9 8                    S          ◇ 7 5
    ♣ K J 2                                ♣ 9 8 7 6 5 4
                        ♠ 7 5 2
                        ♡ A J 10 6 4 3
                        ◇ J 6
                        ♣ Q 10
```

South	West	North	East
2♡	2♠	2NT	3♠
Pass	4♠	6♡!	Pass
Pass	6♠	Pass!	Pass
Dbl.	Pass	7♡	Pass
Pass	Dbl.	Pass	Pass
Pass			

AFTER SOUTH OPENED with a weak 2♡ bid, North "knew" that his side was likely to be cold for a grand slam. The only problem was to avoid the spade sacrifice by his non-vulnerable opponents -- the more so after West's 2♠ overcall. A cue bid would alert the E-W pair to the situation, so he constructed a tactical auction, beginning with a temporizing, though forcing, 2NT overcall. When he finally leapt to 6♡, he had decided to settle for half a loaf if necessary. After all, +1460 for 6♡ making seven is better than +700 for defeating 4♠ doubled. When East bid 6♠, North's pass was forcing. South doubled, and then North bid 7♡. East exceeded North's fondest expectations by doubling. The play was, of course, a pianola. South ruffed the opening lead, pulled trumps in one round, and established the diamonds in dummy with one ruff, making his doubled grand slam. The built-in accuracy of the weak two bid gave North a chance to do some profitable fooling around.

North-South +2470

96

Dealer: South
Vul: East-West

```
                        ♠ K
                        ♡ Q J 10 3
                        ◊ Q 10 3 2
                        ♣ K 10 9 8
        ♠ 10 9 8              N          ♠ 7 5 4
        ♡ A 8 7 5        W         E     ♡ K 6 4 2
        ◊ A J 7 6             S          ◊ K 4
        ♣ A 5                            ♣ Q J 7 6
                        ♠ A Q J 6 3 2
                        ♡ 9
                        ◊ 9 8 5
                        ♣ 4 3 2
```

South	West	North	East
2♠	Dbl.	3♠ !	4♡
Pass	Pass	Dbl.	Pass
Pass	Pass		

THE WEAK TWO BID gives a non-vulnerable pair many ways in which
to take advantage of vulnerable opponents. This hand illustrates the
"pseudo-preempt," a tactical attempt to lead unsuspecting opponents
along the primrose path to destruction. West's take-out double would
be suspect, even at favorable vulnerability. With a minimum hand
and little distribution, he should pass and await developments. Over
North's tactical 3♠ bid, East's 4♡ bid was absolutely correct. He had
a right to expect both a better hand and better distribution from his
partner. After South's trump lead, East had to be careful to avoid
a complete rout. He won the heart in his hand and took the losing
club finesse, before playing a second round of trump. If East had
made the mistake of playing a second round of trump before taking
the club finesse, he would have been held to four tricks, since North
could clear the trump suit, permitting South to cash all his spades.
As it was, the final result was down three -- 800 points for North-
South. "How could you bid 4♡ with that rag?" espostulated West.
"Perhaps you might have more next time you double a weak two bid,"
East replied.

Dealer: West
Vul: None

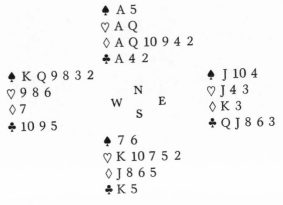

```
                        ♠ A 5
                        ♡ A Q
                        ◊ A Q 10 9 4 2
                        ♣ A 4 2
     ♠ K Q 9 8 3 2              N              ♠ J 10 4
     ♡ 9 8 6              W           E        ♡ J 4 3
     ◊ 7                        S              ◊ K 3
     ♣ 10 9 5                                  ♣ Q J 8 6 3
                        ♠ 7 6
                        ♡ K 10 7 5 2
                        ◊ J 8 6 5
                        ♣ K 5
```

South Romanelli	West Roudinesco	North Loynaz	East Pariente
----	2♠	3♣	3♠
4♡	Pass	Pass	Pass

THE 1967 WORLD CHAMPIONSHIP MATCH between France and Venezuela produced this interesting victory for the weak two bid. At the other table, where the Venezuelan contingent was not playing weak two bids, the North-South French pair of Svarc and Boulenger conducted an undisturbed auction to reach the laydown small slam in diamonds. The French pair, who were playing weak two bids, started the auction preemptively. North's 3♣ call was Fishbein, and East continued the preempt with a 3♠ bid, putting South in an untenable position. He finally decided to bid 4♡, which gave his partner a problem with his 20-point holding. He feared to bid on due to his doubleton heart, since partner might be short in diamonds, in which case either red-suit contract might be in jeopardy at the five level. 4♡ became the final contract, making eleven tricks for +450. In the other room, 6◊ was bid and made for a score of +920. The French gain was directly due to the preemptive value of the weak two bid, since there is no doubt that the Venezuelans would have reached the diamond slam if there were no interference.

Net gain -- 470 points (10 IMP's)

Chapter 5

CONVENTIONAL
VARIANTS

5

NEW CONVENTIONS IN BIDDING COME AND GO, but it seems that the weak two bid is one highly useful and powerful concept that is here to stay. One of the criteria for the projected longevity of any convention is its flexibility. If you have to invent an entirely new system to be able to cope with one new piece of bidding machinery, it usually isn't worth the bother. It should be obvious, however, that whether you play Goren, Roth-Stone, Kaplan-Sheinwold, Precision, Schenken, or most any other system, weak two bids can be incorporated painlessly into your present bidding methods with little or no trouble.

FLANNERY

It is not wholly by accident that two clubs is reserved for the strong hand while diamonds, hearts, and spades describe weak hands. The theory is that since clubs occupy the lowest place in the hierarchy of suit ranking, a weak two club bid would not have much preemptive value and is best used as the catch-all bid for the super-strong hand. William Flannery of Pittsburgh, Pennsylvania, decided that two diamonds has almost the same poor preemptive value as two clubs and proposed the idea of using a two diamond opening to show any hand in the minimum opening range (12-16 HCP) containing precisely five hearts and four spades. Examples of hands that would be opened with a Flannery two diamond bid are:

(a)   ♠ A Q 10 7   (b)   ♠ K 10 5 4
       ♡ K 10 9 8 5   ♡ Q J 5 4 3
       ♢ J 3   ♢ A Q 2
       ♣ K 2   ♣ J

(a) ♠ A Q 10 7　　　(b) ♠ K 10 5 4　　　(c) ♠ A K J 7
♥ K 10 9 8 5　　　♥ Q J 5 4 3　　　♥ A J 9 7 4
♦ J 3　　　　　　♦ A Q 2　　　　♦ 6
♣ K 2　　　　　　♣ J　　　　　　♣ Q 10 9

　　　(d) ♠ J 10 9 4　　　(e) ♠ A J 9 7
♥ K Q J 10 9　　　♥ J 5 4 3 2
♦ A K 9 5　　　　♦ 8
♣ - - -　　　　　♣ A K J

All responses to Flannery are natural, with the exception of two no trump. Before tackling the multifaceted two no trump response, study this schedule of the other responses.

(a) TWO HEARTS or TWO SPADES. A complete denial of any interest in game. Responder may have a bad hand with only three trumps. The two diamond bidder should not bid again, even with a maximum hand.

(b) THREE HEARTS or THREE SPADES. Invitational to game and, of course, non-forcing. The opener should determine whether or not to bid game by the general texture of his trump suit together with his minor suit holding: 3-1 distribution in the minors would be a plus factor while a 2-2 distribution in the minors (especially without a minor suit ace) would be a minus factor.

(c) FOUR HEARTS or FOUR SPADES. "Shut-out" bids. Opener must pass.

(d) THREE CLUBS or THREE DIAMONDS. Non-forcing, though highly invitational, either to three no trump or five of a minor. Responder's hand should contain 10 to 13 HCPs, with a reasonably good six-card suit. Needless to say, this bid denies an eight-card combined holding in either major. With a singleton in partner's suit and a minimum range Flannery bid, opener should pass because of the bad fit. In rare cases, where opener has especially good hearts, he might try bidding that suit in an effort to reach game; e.g.:

♠ K x x x　♥ A K Q 10 x　♦ J 10 x　♣ x

After a three club response to a two diamond opening, opener might try three hearts.

With a doubleton in partner's minor suit, the tendency is to bid three no trump, especially when the doubleton includes a high honor. With three-card support, opener should not hesitate to raise partner.

North
- ♠ 3 2
- ♡ K
- ◇ 7 6 5 4
- ♣ K Q 5 4 3 2

South
- ♠ A K Q 7
- ♡ A 10 9 5 4
- ◇ 3
- ♣ J 9 8

South	North
2 ◇	3 ♣[1]
4 ♣[2]	5 ♣[3]

[1]Showing long clubs with little game interest.

[2]Although partner has denied game interest, possession of three trumps and a singleton diamond are added assets. On this basis, South correctly determined that the hand is worth a game try.*

[3]North decided that his king of hearts was a "working card" and bid and made game, losing one trick in each minor.

*A major suit cuebid might have been more accurate.

(f) TWO NOTRUMP. As in the classic weak two bid, a two notrump bid by responder expresses a desire to find out more information about the general strength and texture of opener's hand. It is forcing and artificial, requesting responder to respond artificially, to show his point count and minor suit distribution.

In response to two notrump, opener describes his strength and minor suit holding according to the following schedule:

(a) Three clubs = 3 clubs, 1 diamond
(b) Three diamonds = 3 diamonds, 1 club
*(c) Three hearts = 2-2 in minors, 11-13 HCPs
*(d) Three spades = 2-2 in minors, 15-16 HCPs
(e) Three notrump = 2-2 in minors with stoppers in both, 14-16 HCPs
(f) Four clubs = 4 clubs and a diamond void
(g) Four diamonds = 4 diamonds and a club void

*14 HCPs may be treated as either minimum range point count or maximum range point count. Examine the texture of your suits, count your ten spots and use your judgment!

(1) THREE CLUBS: A three-card club suit (4-5-1-3 distribution)

(2) THREE DIAMONDS: A three-card diamond suit (4-5-3-1)

(3) THREE HEARTS: 2-2 distribution in the minors and a minimum range hand (12-13 HCPs)

(4) THREE NO TRUMP: 2-2 distribution in the minors and a maximum range hand (14-16 HCPs)

(5) FOUR CLUBS: A four-card club suit (4-5-0-4 distribution)

(6) FOUR DIAMONDS: A four-card diamond suit (4-5-4-0)

Notice the interesting use of three no trump instead of three spades for the fourth responsive step. One reason for this is to allow the unknown hand to become declarer in case the contract ends up in spades. If the Flannery opener should become declarer, especially after an investigatory two no trump sequence, the defenders will know a great deal about the closed hand. A disadvantage to this schedule of responses is that there is no provision made to determine the general high card strength of hands where the opener has a singleton or void in one of the minor suits. With this in mind, and also to provide a use for a three spade response, consider this alternate schedule of rebids found on the convention cards of some experts.

*(1) THREE CLUBS: Minimum range point count (12-13 HCPs) with 2-2 distribution in the minor suits

*(2) THREE DIAMONDS: Minimum range point count (12-13) HCPs) with 3-1 distribution in the minor suits

*(3) THREE HEARTS: Maximum range point count (15-16 HCPs) with 2-2 distribution in the minor suits

*(4) THREE SPADES: Maximum range point count with 3-1 distribution in the minor suits

*(5) THREE NO TRUMP: Any hand with a minor suit void (4-5-0-4 or 4-5-4-0 distribution

If responder now bids three no trump or four of a major, the opening bidder should pass. If, however, responder bids four clubs, he is asking for the location of opener's minor suit shortness. With a singleton or void in diamonds, opener rebids four diamonds, while with a singleton or void in clubs, opener rebids four hearts. Please

---

*14 HCPs may be treated as either minimum range point count or maximum range point count. Examine the texture of your suits, count your ten spots and use your judgment!

(c)

♠ Q J 10 9 8
♡ 2
◇ A 10 5 4 3
♣ 3 2

FOUR SPADES. Take your chances and leap to four spades. Partner is likely to have a singleton diamond and you might be able to make ten tricks on a red-suit cross-ruff without even breathing hard. An invitational bid of three spades would be cowardly.

(d)

♠ K 3 2
♡ 9
◇ A 9 8 7 6 3
♣ J 6 3

TWO SPADES. A sign-off bid of two spades is the proper call on this hand. While the hand may make a lucky game in diamonds if partner has a perfect fit, he is just as likely to have diamond shortness in which case you may end up in an unmakable contract. On this basis, contracting for eight tricks is your best chance for a plus score.

(e)

♠ Q 5
♡ J 9
◇ A K Q J 3 2
♣ Q J 2

TWO NOTRUMP. The most likely contract will be three notrump since, as in the previous example, partner would need some sort of magic hand for slam. We recommend, however, that you try a forcing bid of two notrump first. If partner shows a singleton club, prospects for slam will become brighter, assuming he holds the necessary control cards. To illustrate, partner's hand might be:

♠ K 9 4 2
♡ A Q 8 6 4
◇ 10
♣ K 9 7

in which case three notrump is right, or partner's hand might be:

♠ A K 4 2
♡ A 7 6 4 2
◇ 9 8 7
♣ K

in which case six diamonds is a laydown.

Declarer	Responder
2◊	2NT
3♣ [1]	4NT
5◊	6♠

while the second schedule of responses might take the slightly longer route of:

Declarer	Responder
2◊	2NT
3◊ [2]	4♣ [3]
4◊ [4]	4NT
5◊	6♠

Whichever method of approach you elect to use, it is clear that this excellent sounding slam based on an obviously splendid fit (minor suit losers should disappear on dummy's long hearts) was easy to reach by use of the Flannery convention.

---

[1] Showing a three-card suit, hence a singleton diamond.
[2] Showing a minimum point count with 3-1 distribution in the minors.
[3] Requesting opener to define his singleton.
[4] Showing a singleton diamond.

(b)
♠ K 3
♡ 6
◊ K Q 10 9 8
♣ A K 9 5 4

TWO NO TRUMP. Again two no trump is the proper call, but for different reasons. If opener's response indicates 3-1 minor suit distribution, a minor suit game or slam should be sought because lack of communication might make three no trump a difficult contract. If opener shows 2-2 distribution in the minors, we should bid three no trump in the expectation of running one of the minors. If opener shows a minor suit void, there is a very real possibility of at least a small slam. It would be a mistake to bid three clubs or three diamonds over partner's two diamond opener, since this would be non-forcing and the hand is much too strong to make a non-forcing bid.

South	North
2 ◇	3 ◇
3 ♡	3 ♠
4 ◇	4 ♡
5 ♡	6 ♣
6 ♡	7 ♠

After North's three diamond bid, South's three heart rebid is forced. Three spades fixes the trump suit and asks for a cuebid. South complies with four diamonds and after North cuebids the ace of hearts, South shows his king of hearts. North's six club cuebid is clearly a sign of interest in a grand slam. South announces the queen of hearts, surely a strong card opposite partner's ace. North correctly reasons that South would not have shown interest in a grand slam without the king of trumps and bids the excellent grand slam in spades.

North
♠ Q 7
♡ A Q 8 5
◇ A 9 8
♣ A 10 8 7

South
♠ J 10 5 4
♡ K J 10 9 7
◇ K Q J
♣ J

South	North
2 ◇	3 ◇
3 ♡	4 ♣
4 ♡	4 NT
5 ◇	5 ♡
Pass	

A slam convention can be used to stay out of bad slams as well as to bid good ones. North's four clubs is a cuebid, fixing hearts as trumps. With no ace to show, South retreats to four hearts. North's four notrump is not ace asking since North already knows that South is aceless. Rather, it asks South for added information. South shows his diamond concentration of strength; North, with two

The obvious advantage of Flannery is that it solves the headaches that sometimes arise with 4-5 major suit distributions, because good game contracts based on "fit" can be reached with a minimum of difficulty. In return for this, you lose the advantages of the weak two diamond bid. Some experienced partnerships who play Flannery solve this dilemma by opening three clubs and three diamonds with hands of "weak two bid" texture. This is largely a matter of style and personal preference. The main point is simple: If you agree with Mr. Flannery's idea of the weak two diamond bid not being terribly useful from a preemptive point of view, it may pay to consider adopting the Flannery two diamond convention.

FLANNERY TWO HEARTS

A minor variant of the Flannery concept is the two heart opening bid which is used by partnerships who open two diamonds with other types of hands--most commonly, the scientific and highly complex Blue Team two diamond opening, which shows 17 or more HCPs, and 4-4-4-1 distribution. The Flannery two heart bid shows the same hand as the Flannery two diamond bid (five hearts and four spades) and the responses and rebids are the same. It is our belief that any advantage gained by using the two heart opening in this manner is lost by not having the two heart bid available as a weak two bid. Thus, despite the fact that we see logic to the argument against the weak two diamond bid (i.e., its lack of preemptive quality), we most emphatically believe in both the aggressive and preemptive value of the weak two bid in both majors. In other words, if you like Flannery two diamonds, it is available; if you like the Blue Team two diamond bid (which is primarily useful in total point or IMP scoring), use it, but don't sacrifice the weak two heart bid for Flannery.

*   *   *

If you have decided that you would like to attempt mastering the nuances of the Flannery two diamond opening, attempt the following quiz on Flannery. Even if you make a couple of errors, but still understand the answers, you are ready to play this convention.

quality), we most emphatically believe in both the aggressive and preemptive value of the weak two bid in both majors. In other words, if you like Flannery two diamonds, it is available; if you like the Blue Team two diamond bid (which is primarily useful in total point or IMP scoring), use it, but don't sacrifice the weak two heart bid for Flannery.

The obvious advantage of Flannery is that it solves the headaches that sometimes arise with 4-5 major suit distributions, because good game contracts based on "fit" can be reached with a minimum of difficulty. In return for this, you lose the advantages of the weak two diamond bid. Some experienced partnerships who play Flannery solve this dilemma by opening three clubs and three diamonds with hand of "weak two bid" texture. This is largely a matter of style and personal preference. The main point is simple: If you agree with Flannery's idea of the weak two diamond bid not being terribly useful from a preemptive point of view, it may pay to consider adopting the Flannery two diamond convention.

If you have decided that you would like to attempt mastering the nuances of the Flannery two diamond opening, try the following quiz on Flannery. Even if you make a couple of errors, but still understand the answers, you are ready to play this convention.

QUIZ ON CHAPTER FIVE

YOU HAVE OPENED THE AUCTION with a Flannery two diamond bid. Partner has responded with two notrump. What would you rebid on each of these hands?

1. ♠ A Q 10 4
   ♡ K Q 10 5 3
   ◇ Q 7 6
   ♣ 5

2. ♠ K Q 7 5
   ♡ A Q 5 3 2
   ◇ A J
   ♣ 10 7

3. ♠ Q J 10 9
   ♡ A K Q J 3
   ◇ J 10 2
   ♣ 5

4. ♠ Q J 7 4
   ♡ K Q 5 4 2
   ◇ K J
   ♣ K 9

5. ♠ A K J 10
   ♡ Q 9 8 5 4
   ◇ —
   ♣ A J 10 9

6. ♠ K J 9 3
   ♡ A Q J 5 4
   ◇ J 2
   ♣ Q 3

2.

♠ K Q 7 5
♡ A Q 5 3 2
◇ A J
♣ 10 7

THREE HEARTS. Showing a maximum strength hand (15-16 HCP) with 2-2 minor suit distribution. The correct bid utilizing the second set of responses is three no trump, again showing a 4-5-2-2 with a maximum strength hand. Notice that both responding methods describe strength and distribution when the minors are divided 2-2.

3.

♠ Q J 10 9
♡ A K Q J 3
◇ J 10 2
♣ 5

THREE SPADES. With 14 HCPs, we must use our judgment on whether to show minimum or maximum strength. Here, the texture of our major suits is excellent and our spot cards are good; hence we consider three spades, showing a maximum range opening with 3-1 minor suit distribution to be the correct response, while three diamonds would be incorrect since it shows a minimum. The first schedule of responses indicates a three diamond rebid, showing a three-card diamond fragment without consideration of the HCPs.

4.

♠ K Q 7 4
♡ J 5 4 3 2
◇ A Q 2
♣ Q

THREE DIAMONDS. As in the last problem, we have 14 HCPs and must use our judgment as to whether this hand is maximum or minimum. We have poor major suit spot cards (especially in hearts) and two of our HCPs are represented by a singleton queen of clubs, certainly not an asset. Compare the general texture of this 14 point hand with #3, which also contained 14 HCPs, but was treated as a maximum. Under the first set of responses, three diamonds is correct, showing a three-card diamond suit.

5.

♠ A K J 10
♡ Q 9 8 5 4
◇ - - -
♣ A J 10 9

THREE NO TRUMP. Showing a void in one of the minors and a four-card holding in the other. Partner will no doubt be interested in the location of your void and will bid four clubs to which you will respond four diamonds, showing a diamond void. (If your void were in clubs, your response would be four hearts). Utilizing the first set of responses,

4.
♠ Q J 7 4
♡ K Q 5 4 2
◇ K J
♣ K 9

THREE NOTRUMP. A descriptive bid showing stoppers in both minors with a healthy opening bid. Responder may pass or correct to a major suit, but whatever happens, you've told your story.

5.
♠ A K J 10
♡ Q 9 8 5 4
◇ —
♣ A J 10 9

FOUR CLUBS. Showing a four-card club suit (hence a diamond void). Partner's reaction to this descriptive information will depend on the location of his minor suit high cards. As an example, holding:

♠ Q 9 7 4   ♡ A 6   ◇ K Q 8 7   ♣ 7 8 3
he would pull in his horns and bid four spades, since his wasted diamond values are a definite disadvantage. But reverse the minors:

♠ Q 9 7 4   ♡ A 6   ◇ 7 6 3   ♣ K Q 8 7
and his hand has grown dramatically in potential. With all cards "working" he might well move towards a small slam in spades.

6.
♠ K J 9 3
♡ A Q J 5 4
◇ J 2
♣ Q 3

THREE HEARTS. We are faced with the problem of deciding whether to treat a 14 HCP hand as minimum or maximum. We lean toward the conservative view in this case because of our lack of minor suit control cards. If you elected to take the aggressive course and bid three spades, because of your good hearts and spades, it would not be strictly incorrect. Remember, 14 HCP hands are a matter of judgment and here, the judgment is close.

7.
♠ A J 7 2
♡ K J 9 3 2
◇ K J 2
♣ 10

PASS. Remember, three clubs is non-forcing, and this minimum hand, lacking a club fit, is the worst we could hold for partner. Be thankful that the singleton club is a ten spot. It may enable partner to make three clubs.

9.
♠ A K 10 7
♡ J 9 7 5 3
◊ A
♣ K 10 7

THREE DIAMONDS. The master bid! Our hand is tremendous opposite partner's three club response and we believe a simple four club raise would not do it justice. Partner's heart holding is the key to a small slam or even a grand slam in clubs. Admittedly, the three diamond bid might be somewhat ambiguous, but since it must be forcing, a later club raise will clarify the fact that we were cue-bidding our diamond control preparatory to supporting partner's club suit.

10.
♠ K Q 10 3
♡ A 10 9 7 6
◊ K 6
♣ Q 9

THREE NO TRUMP. Our Q x of clubs should enable us to run the entire suit unless something evil happens, and since we have a "medium strength" two diamond opener, there should be a good play for nine tricks. Notice that it is important that we play the hand so that the lead will come up to our K x of diamonds.

11.
♠ A J 4 2
♡ K Q 5 4 3
◊ 7
♣ A 8 7

FOUR CLUBS. The classic hand with which to make this non-forcing though highly invitational raise. The possession of control cards plus a singleton diamond makes five clubs a very possible contract. If partner is looking at a hand with unfortunate diamond duplication, e.g.

 ♠ 4 3 ♡ J 2 ◊ K J 8 ♣ K Q 10 9 3 2

he can pass.

12.
♠ A 9 7 6
♡ A K Q 10 9
◊ 3 2
♣ K 2

THREE HEARTS. This very good hand presents a difficult rebid problem. Clearly, three no trump is unbiddable from our side -- the whole diamond suit could easily be wide open and the auction screams for a diamond lead. We don't want to pass with our 16 HCPs and we can't raise clubs with 2-2 distribution in the minor suits. The three heart bid should show an interest in a heart game opposite two little hearts (indicating a solid or semi-solid suit). If partner rebids three no trump you should pass, while if partner bids four clubs, you should raise to five clubs.

INTERMEDIATE (ACOL) TWO BIDS

For those bridge players who scorn opening a two bid with a weak hand but at the same time recognize the impracticality of reserving the entire two level for super-powerful hands that occur very rarely, the intermediate two bid may be a practical compromise.

The intermediate two bid is no newcomer to bridge. Developed in the early 1930's, it has become an essential ingredient of the Acol system as well as other "light initial action" systems.

Simply stated, an opening bid of two diamonds, two hearts, or two spades shows a strong distributional hand with at least eight playing tricks. Ideally, the hand should contain a very good six-card or longer suit with at least one outside control, although it is permissible to have two strong five-card suits. Some examples of hands that would be opened with an intermediate two bid are:

(a) ♠ A Q 3
♡ A K J 10 5 4
◊ Q J 3
♣ 9
(17 HCPs)

(b) ♠ A K Q 10 9 8 7
♡ 2
◊ 8 5
♣ A J 7
(14 HCPs)

(c) ♠ A K Q 5 4 3
♡ K Q J 9 8
◊ 7
♣ 4
(15 HCPs)

(d) ♠ A 2
♡ A 2
◊ A K Q 5 4 3
♣ J 5 2
(18 HCPs)

(e) ♠ K Q J
♡ A Q J 10 9 5 4 3 2
◊ - - -
♣ 2
(13 HCPs)

Please notice that the theme of the intermediate two bid is trick-taking potential and not HCPs. Hand (d) contains 18 HCPs, while hand (e) contains merely 13 HCPs, yet both hands have an eight trick potential opposite a flat Yarborough. For the magnificient hands with a plethora of high cards and controls, the strong, forcing and artificial two club bid is still used.

RESPONSES: In its original design, an opening intermediate two bid was non-forcing though highly invitational. When this bid was incorporated into the Acol structure, it became 100% forcing for one round and while some experts still play intermediate two bids in the old-fashioned non-forcing way, most utilize Acol methods of response.

The philosophy of Acol is "natural bidding" with a minimum of artificialities, and the Acol two bid is no exception. As in the strong two bid, a two no trump response is negative, while all other bids are natural and game forcing. One important point that must be considered, however, when comparing the Acol two bid with the super-strong two bid is that an Acol two bid is often employed with a minimum HCP range hand and it is quite possible that responder will have a good share of the honor cards. As an example, suppose you held:

♠ 5 3   ♡ K J 7 2   ◊ Q J 4   ♣ Q 9 7 3

You are playing strong two bids and partner opens two spades. Your thinking with your 9 HCPs would be slam-oriented and you would endeavor to convey this to partner by whatever means you have available. Playing Acol two bids, however, your correct response would be 2NT (negative), planning to raise partner's expected rebid of three spades to game (and rebid three no trump over anything else) in the hope that game can be made. This means that the negative response to an Acol two bid is often made with a stronger hand than the negative response to a strong two bid. Keeping in mind that he can have a pretty good hand for a negative 2NT response to an Acol two bid, it follows that a new suit by responder should be based on a better hand. As a general rule, a new suit by responder should be a five-card holding or better, with at least the HCP strength required by Standard American bidding methods for a two-over-one response to an opening bid. If responder should be fortunate enough to hold a solid suit of his own, he shows this by making a single jump in his suit. Your partner will now know that with two strong suits between you, a zillion tricks are available and either Blackwood or control-showing cue bids would be appropriate to investigate slam possibilities.

The only other consideration for responder is the direct raise of partner's suit. An immediate raise to game is a "shut-out" bid denying any interest in slam exploration. A single raise of partner's suit, on the other hand, is one of the strongest bids available to responder. It shows a definite interest in slam and asks opener to show control cards outside of his suit. Opener can cue-bid an ace if he has one, or bid 3NT without an ace.

Reviewing the responses to an Acol two bid, the partner of the two bidder may:

1. Bid two no trump (negative response)
2. Bid a new suit
   (a) At the cheapest level (10 or more HCPs and a five-card suit)
   (b) Jumping one level (showing a solid suit)
3. Raise partner's suit
   (a) To game (a sign-off)
   (b) One level (showing slam interest)

Examine each of the following six hands. Partner has opened the bidding with an Acol two heart bid, What is your response?

(a) ♠ J 10 8 4 3 2   (b) ♠ A 5 4 2   (c) ♠ K 4 3
    ♡ 7 6   ♡ Q 7   ♡ 5
    ◊ K J 4   ◊ A K Q J 3   ◊ A 10 3 2
    ♣ Q 4   ♣ J 9   ♣ K Q 10 9 7

            (d) ♠ J 9 8 3 2   (e) ♠ A 4
                ♡ 10   ♡ K Q 10
                ◊ Q 5 3   ◊ 5 4 3 2
                ♣ 5 4 3 2   ♣ K J 4 3

ANSWERS

(a)
♠ J 10 8 4 3 2
♡ 7 6
◊ K J 4
♣ Q 4

TWO NO TRUMP. It would be an error to bid two spades. With 7 HCPs the first obligation to partner is to describe a negative holding by bidding two no trump. If partner rebids three hearts, simply bid game in hearts. If, however, the hand is changed to:

♠ J 10 8 4 3 2   ♡ 7   ◊ K J 4   ♣ Q 6 4

it would pay to try three spades over partner's three heart rebid. Partner may have a doubleton honor in spades in which case he should bid four spades. If, instead, partner retreats to four hearts, your diamond and club holding may be enough to produce a game.

115

(b)

♠ A 5 4 2
♡ Q 7
◇ A K Q J 3
♣ J 9

THREE HEARTS. Three hearts, the strongest response, should be the call on this strong hand. A jump in diamonds showing a solid suit is unnecessary, since the Q 7 of hearts should solidify partner's suit. The key to the hand is partner's club holding, which will determine whether the hand should be played at the five, six or seven level. If you've agreed to play ace-showing bids over the single raise and partner bids four clubs showing the ace of clubs, you should leap directly to a grand slam in no trump since you can virtually count thirteen tricks. If, on the other hand, partner bids three no trump or four hearts showing no ace outside of the heart suit, bid four spades. Partner should show second round control in clubs if he has it, in which case six hearts or six no trump is cold from his side of the table. If partner does not show a second round club control, stop at five hearts. His hand probably looks like:

♠ K Q J ♡ A K J 10 9 8 2 ◇ 5 ♣ Q 8

in which case the hand is off two club tricks. As many points are lost bidding unmakable slams as are lost not reaching cold slams!

(c)

♠ K 4 3
♡ 5
◇ A 10 3 2
♣ K Q 10 9 7

THREE CLUBS. The proper call on this hand with a five-card suit and better than ten HCPs. If partner has the right cards, slam is not out of the question. If he has the wrong hand, 3NT or four hearts should be simple enough.

(d)

♠ J 9 8 3 2
♡ 10
◇ Q 5 3
♣ 5 4 3 2

TWO NO TRUMP. Two no trump is obviously the proper bid, planning to pass partner's expected three heart rebid. Strangely enough, if partner had opened his two bid in any other suit, we would be tempted to press on to game on the strength of our singleton heart, which is now a liability.

(e)

♠ A 4
♡ K Q 10
◇ 5 4 3 2
♣ K J 4 3

Since partner cannot have an Acol two bid when you have the K Q 10 of his trump suit, try to remember what you and he used to play and respond accordingly. He's forgotten that you've agreed to play intermediate two bids with him!

While hand (e) was meant to be amusing, it also serves to reinforce a particular requirement of this type of two bid -- the suit must be of excellent quality, certainly no worse than A Q J x x x. Used accurately, the Acol two bid can be a useful weapon. Abuse the Acol two bid and it may very well come back to haunt you in the form of a terrible bidding disaster!

OPENER'S REBIDS

We have already learned that the Acol opening two bid shows a minimum of about eight playing tricks. It can be quite a bit stronger, however. Consider the following hand:

♠ A Q J 10 9 7 3 2 ♡ - - - ◇ K Q 10 9 ♣ 2

Despite the fact that this exciting array contains over nine playing tricks, you would not open the auction with a forcing two club bid, since you have only 13 HCP. Two spades is the proper call, planning to jump the bidding on the next round to differentiate between this hand and a less shapely one such as:

♠ A K Q 9 8 7 ♡ 7 ◇ A Q 5 4 ♣ 8 3

To further illustrate this principle, notice the dramatic auction on this hand:

♠ - - - ♡ A K 9 8 5 4 ◇ 3 ♣ A K 6 5 4 2

South	West	North	East
2♡	Pass	2NT	Pass
6♣!!	Pass	Pass	Pass

South decided to take his chances by bidding the slam despite the negative response by partner. Even if the dummy produced a complete Yarborough, three small cards in either of South's long suits plus a 2-2 trump break would give a good chance to establish the other long suit with a ruff.

Since the Acol opening two bid shows as few as eight playing tricks, it is not forcing to game, since partner will often hold an assortment of useless cards. Consider:

♠ A K Q 10 7 6 ♡ A Q 10 2 ◊ K 7 ♣ 5

This is a nice hand...a very nice hand, but not enough to guarantee game. If partner responds two no trump after you open the auction with two spades, your correct bid is three spades, knowing that partner will bid game on any excuse.

In general, after a two no trump response, opener can bid game on a hand which he feels is strong enough to make game opposite any possible holding by partner, or he can invite game by either rebidding his original suit or showing a second suit. He can also force responder to bid again by making a jump rebid in his second suit, if the jump is short of the game level.

* * * *

While we accept the fact that many excellent contracts can be reached via the intermediate two bid route, these results can usually be achieved by standard bidding methods. Therefore, we do not believe that it compensates for the loss of the weak two bid (especially in the majors). Even in "Acol-land" there are those who recognize the potency of the weak two bid, such as Scottish champion Albert L. Benjamin, who has devised a system of two bids whereby Acol players could have their cake and their weak two bids in the majors too. An opening bid of two clubs, according to Mr. Benjamin, shows an Acol two bid in an unspecified suit. A two diamond response is negative after which opener shows his suit with a non-forcing, natural call. A two diamond opening now becomes the strong, game forcing, artificial bid, while two hearts and two spades are free to do their duty as weak two bids. We believe this to be a highly intelligent and theoretically sound way to treat two-level auctions. Who knows? It may be the system of the future!

Chapter 6

MORE ADVANCED CONCEPTS

Chapter 9

SOME ADVANCED CONCEPTS

6

VERY EARLY IN THIS BOOK, we noted that one of the virtues of the strong two club bid is that it frees the other three suits for use of the weak two bid. After reading Chapter III, the alert reader doubtless noticed that we assigned no meaning to a two no trump opening bid. Most partnerships use a direct two no trump opening to show a hand with 21-22 high card points or even a very good 20 points. Examine the following four hands:

(a) ♠ A Q	(b) ♠ A K 5 4	(c) ♠ A K 9	(d) ♠ Q 4 3
♡ K Q 7 5	♡ Q J 8 6	♡ Q J 10 6	♡ A Q J
◇ K Q 5 3	◇ A K 2	◇ A Q 10	◇ A K Q 6
♣ K Q 10	♣ A J	♣ A 10 8	♣ Q 8 7
(21 pts.)	(22 pts.)	(20 pts.)	(20 Pts.)

Hands (a) and (b) contain 21 and 22 high card points respectively and under these methods should be opened with two no trump. This defines a hand that is not quite strong enough to open the bidding with two clubs, but is strong enough to desire a game with very little in partner's hand. Hand (c) should also be opened with two no trump, despite the fact that it contains only 20 high card points. The possession of the many "spot cards" adds a great deal to the playing strength. Hand (d) contains 20 high card points also, but should not be opened two no trump. Not only are there weaknesses in the black suits, but the hand contains no tens or nines. This kind of a hand should be opened with one diamond, planning to rebid two no trump, which shows a hand containing 18 to 20 high card points.

Some of the younger theoreticians have found an even more interesting use for the two no trump opening bid, treating it as the unusual no trump, asking for a response in the better minor suit. This opening bid is even more effective than the conventional use of the unusual two no trump overcall, since the opponents do not know anything about each other's hands. As an example, assume that your partner has passed and your right hand opponent has passed. You have the following hand:

♠ 5   ♡ 4 2   ◇ K J 8 6 3   ♣ K Q J 4 2

You have only 10 high card points, and it is likely that the opponents have a major suit fit. By opening the bidding with two no trump (unusual) you may stymie your left hand opponent who is doubtless looking at a good one heart or one spade opening bid. You have told your story to your partner with one bid, and he may now act accordingly. While we do not necessarily recommend this use of the two no trump opening bid, it is certainly an interesting idea, and just one more example of the flexibility available to us.

THE JACOBY TRANSFER BID

In Chapter III we showed that there are times when the weaker hand would like to indicate a suit to the stronger hand. The theoretical purpose of the Jacoby Transfer Bid is to make the strong hand declarer and keep it concealed from the opponents. In addition, the Jacoby transfer allows responder to describe his distribution with great ease and accuracy. The theory involved is quite sound and Jacoby is a very useful tool.

The Jacoby transfer is used in three different situations:
1. After a one no trump opening bid.
2. After a two no trump opening bid.
3. After a two club opening bid followed by a two diamond (negative) response and a two no trump rebid by opener.

Within the framework of this book, our concern is with two club and two no trump openings. Simply stated, the responder to the two no trump bid (or rebid) would show a major suit, five cards or longer, by bidding the suit directly beneath his five card holding. Thus, a three diamond bid would show five or more hearts and would request partner to bid hearts, while a three heart bid would show five or more spades and request partner to bid spades. (To investigate a minor-suit fit, responder bids three spades, requesting partner to bid a four card minor if he has one, and to bid no trump if he does not have a four card minor.)

With this in mind, assume you are holding the following:

♠ K 9 8 5 3   ♡ K 7 6   ◇ 4 2   ♣ 6 5 3

Partner opens the bidding with two clubs, you respond with a negative two diamonds (six evaluated points), and partner rebids two no trump. The proper rebid on this hand would be a Jacoby transfer bid of three hearts, telling your partner you have five or more spades. After partner's three spade bid (remember, he is forced to respond in spades), you bid three no trump. Now partner knows that you have between three and seven high card points, exactly five spades and no other suit to show. On the basis of this information, he can decide whether to play three no trump or four spades. Note: If responder has more than five spades, he would correct from three no trump to four spades, since he knows that opener has at least a doubleton spade. A fringe benefit of this method is that if responder wishes to stop short of game, he can simply transfer to his major then pass!

We have stated that the opening bidder is compelled to rebid in the requested suit, but he is allowed some freedom of action, depending on whether he has a minimum or maximum hand in support of partner's indicated suit, based entirely upon the fit in the suit. With a minimum the opener merely responds on the same level as the transfer; with a maximum and a fit, he jumps one level in the requested suit. Consider the following two hands:

	(a)		(b)
	♠ A Q 5 4		♠ A 3
	♡ K 5 2		♡ K Q 6 4
	◇ A K 7		◇ A Q J 3
	♣ A K 9		♣ A K 9

The first four bids on each hand are identical -- you open the bidding two clubs and, over partner's two diamond response, rebid two no trump. In each case, partner has rebid three hearts, requesting you to bid spades. With the first hand, your holding is considerably improved by the spade fit, so a four spade bid is correct, not three spades, since the established fit forecasts a play for game even with a very poor dummy. The second hand is not good support for partner's suit and the opening bidder should content himself with a three spade response. Notice that both hands have the identical 23 high card points, yet the first hand justifies an aggressive action, while the second hand does not. This is based only on the trump fit since you have already announced an excellent hand by opening the bidding with two clubs.

Examine the following hands:

	(a)		(b)		(c)
	♠ K 7 5 4 2		♠ Q 8 6 5 4 3		♠ K 5 4 2
	♡ 3		♡ 3		♡ Q J 8 6 5
	◇ 8 2		◇ K 6 4 3 2		◇ 2
	♣ K 5 4 3 2		♣ 4		♣ 6 4 3

In each case, partner has opened the bidding with two clubs and, over your two diamond response, has rebid two no trump. What is your plan for the auction? On hand (a) you should rebid three hearts, forcing partner to bid spades. If he bids three spades, you should bid four clubs, showing him your second suit and a distributional hand. If he bids four spades over your original transfer bid in hearts, you should consider trying for a slam. On hand (b) you should also bid three hearts for transfer; if partner responds with three spades, you should bid four spades, while if partner responds four spades, you should consider slam because of your unusual distribution. On hand (c) you should bid three diamonds, transferring to hearts; if partner bids four hearts, you pass, while if partner bids three hearts you bid three spades, indicating a five card heart suit and a four card (or longer) spade suit. Notice how simply your distribution is described, and notice how much information is exchanged at a low level. An alternate method of describing this hand would be to employ the Stayman convention, (3♣ asking for the majors), but we believe that the use of the Jacoby convention most accurately describes our askew distribution.

A basic rule of Jacoby is that a new suit by the transferrer is forcing and shows a good hand. Consider this auction:

South	West	North	East
2NT	Pass	3♡	Pass
3♠	Pass	4◊	Pass
?			

Four diamonds is a forcing bid showing at least nine cards, possibly more, in the spade and diamond suits. It would not be logical for North to have gone through this descriptive process unless he was interested in game or slam.

This convention is ideally suited to a two suited hand, as illustrated in several of the preceding examples. Consider this hand:

♠ 4 2   ♡ K 8 6 4 2   ◊ K J 4 3 2   ♣ 5

Partner opens with two clubs and over your two diamond response, he rebids no trump. If you are playing Jacoby transfers, you indicate your heart suit by bidding diamonds, then rebid diamonds to show five-five distribution or better. You are certain that game is in hand, and partner can determine slam possibilities if the hands fit well, despite your paucity of high cards.

The only other rule to remember about Jacoby transfers is that, like all other artificial bids, it is not used in a competitive auction. If the opponents enter the bidding, all bids become natural.

Like any other bidding tool, Jacoby requires some practice to use effectively. After a short while it becomes easy and will reward you with superior contracts played from the strong hand.

PRE-EMPTIVE JUMP OVERCALLS

Many partnerships use weak jump overcalls as part of their bidding methods -- if the opponents open the bidding, a single jump in a new suit is preemptive, that is, a long suit with less than an opening bid. A good rule of thumb to use is that a preemptive jump overcall is basically the same hand with which you would open a weak two bid, dependent on vulnerability, suit texture, high card strength and so on, and the same responding methods can be used. Thus, given the following:

♠ A Q 7 5 4 2   ♡ K 4 2   ◊ 5 2   ♣ 8 6

If the right hand opponent opens the bidding with one heart, a two spade bid shows a hand that is equivalent to a weak two bid. Partnew can then bid a new suit (forcing), he can use a two no trump bid to start an Ogust sequence, or employ any of the other tools of the weak two bid itself.

INTO THE NINETIES - AN OVERVIEW

Throughout the last half a century, the weak two bid has proved to be as useful a weapon as any in the average player's arsenal. There is no doubt about it; the weak two bid is here to stay. Over the years competitors have fine-tuned the weak two to suit their personal needs, and in this section we'll relate these adjustments to the five rules and regulations of the classic weak two bid:

A. The suit should be six cards long.
B. The strength should be between six and twelve HCP's.
C. A maximum of one outside ace or king.
D. The hand should not contain a void.
E. No outside four card major.

With minor exceptions, these rules have stood the test of time. Some new approaches call for slightly lighter opening bids and in these cases, the six to twelve HCP range can be replaced by five to eleven HCP's. For the same reason, some light initial action partnerships consider an outside ace or king to be a negative factor. These adjustments are, or should be, the rough extent of the weak two evolution, but there are those who feel a compelling need to reinvent the wheel.

As with any other bidding method, players have explored various corruptions of the classical weak two bid, attaching that most frightening appellation, "modified". We have experienced modified Precision, modified negative doubles and even modified Blackwood; why not modified weak two bids?

The current vogue among a minority group of experts is the weak weak two bid based on a five card suit (maybe), five or six high card points (maybe), and a fair degree of unmitigated gall. The convention card depiction for this approach would be "highly undisciplined", and it has become S.O.P. to employ the weak two bid with something like:

a. ♠Kxxxxx ♥Jxx ♦xxx ♣x
b. ♠xx ♥AQxxx ♦xxx ♣xxx.
c. ♠void ♥Qxxxxx ♦ QT9xx ♣xx
d. ♠Jxxxx ♥Qxxx ♦xx ♣xx

In each of the above hands there is at least one weak two bid rule violation.

Hand (a) is the closest to a classic two bid. The suit is a little too weak and four HCP's are outside the minimum range; but not vulnerable versus vulnerable opponents, it is close to an acceptable gamble. Hand (b) is marginal in third chair. In any other seat it is tactical rather than descriptive in nature.

Hand (c) abuses almost every concept of the weak two bid. Except for the six card suit, it bears scarce resemblance to a weak two. It is not strong enough; there is a second five card suit and a void. Plus, it provides no lead directing assistance. If (c) is bad, (d) should be banned—not enough suit, an outside four card major, and not enough strength.

None of this it would be so terrible if the proponents of these methods kept their opinions to themselves. Alas, they seem compelled to proselytize. Admiring students are taught not only that these are acceptable two bids, but that it would be incorrect not to open them. While writing this section, the following hand came up in a flighted mixed pairs.

North-South Vulnerable

```
                    ♠ AQ9732
                    ♥ T6
                    ♦ 98
                    ♣ K97
    ♠ JT865                         ♠ K
    ♥ J7                            ♥ K8542
    ♦ J542                          ♦ A76
    ♣ AT                            ♣ Q865
                    ♠ 4
                    ♥ AQ93
                    ♦ KQT3
                    ♣ J432
```

North	East	South	West
			2S!
Pass	Pass	Dbl	Pass
Pass	Pass		

After West opened with a "modern" weak two bid, the auction was automatic; North converted South's take out double for penalties. Although my partner and I did not defend perfectly (we only beat it 4 tricks), this coldest of tops created a not-very-friendly discussion between the opponents. Finally, they asked for our opinion of West's opening bid. My partner tried the tactful approach.

"Not quite a lead directing bid," my partner observed.

"That wasn't lead directing, stupid", snapped West, "it was a weak two bid..."

Most players who employ the "weak" weak two bid overlook the fact that they lose the aggressive accuracy found in the classic weak two. Partner no longer has the ability to determine the likelihood of game, the profitability of a sacrifice, or determine his partnership's combined defensive capabilities. The main value of this "modern" tendency is to steal from weak or inexperienced players. This is counterproductive, because the weaker pairs' best chance happens when the auction becomes sufficiently clouded or the contract sufficiently weird to·frustrate the possibility of a normal result. Therefore, it must be in the stronger player's best interest to have clear definitions of what makes up a weak two bid. The following hand is from a New England knockout match. North-South were members of the stronger team. Had they followed the normal winning procedure of superior cool headed technique, the issue would never have been in doubt, but they decided to confuse their opponents with an orgy of fancy bidding.

North-South Vulnerable.

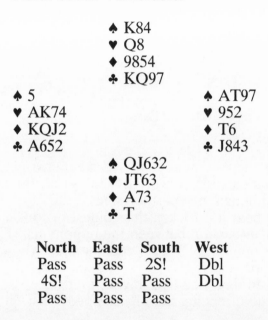

	♠ K84	
	♥ Q8	
	♦ 9854	
	♣ KQ97	
♠ 5		♠ AT97
♥ AK74		♥ 952
♦ KQJ2		♦ T6
♣ A652		♣ J843
	♠ QJ632	
	♥ JT63	
	♦ A73	
	♣ T	

North	East	South	West
Pass	Pass	2S!	Dbl
4S!	Pass	Pass	Dbl
Pass	Pass	Pass	

At unfavorable vulnerability, South's opening bid is criminal and will lose more often then it gains. North completed the farce with an intimidating leap to four spades after West's double. West doubled again, and of course, East had no problem passing for penalties. The play was foolproof—East-West took two spades, two hearts, two diamonds and a club for +1100. Needless to say, North-South's teammates were not overjoyed when West brought in a close 3NT at the other table for +400 and a thirteen IMP loss. An unlucky hand? Not really. South opened the door to disaster. The opponents merely garnered the fruits.

Since the undisciplined two bid is a losing tactic, the obvious question is, why do it? The answer is psychological rather than bridge related. There are some players who would rather win 20 IMPs by bravado then 100 IMPs by straightforward play. There are weaker players who conceal a lack of actual ability with flair and clamor, and there are people who get their jollies by trying to humiliate the opposition. Whatever the reason, it is predictably bad bridge and certainly bad manners.

Undisciplined weak two bids lead to a more delicate problem. Tournament players know that the rules are precise about all opposing partnership agreements. If a player can open a weak two bid with three points or eleven points, there is likely to be a tacit agreement regarding what specific conditions are likely to trigger a "weak" weak two. Whether these conditions are vulnerability, state of the match or anything else, it is against both the letter and spirit of the law. The ACBL agreed, and for a long time weak two's with less than 5 HCP's, suits less than 5 cards long, or a range of more than 7 HCP's were illegal. In 1987, the League rescinded this regulation in order to deal directly with the problem of private partnership understandings. Undisciplined or irregular weak two's are now allowed, but conventional responses to determine the degree of irregularity are not. In order to be able to use conventional responses the range for a weak two must fall into either 5-11 HCP's, 6-12 HCP's, or 7-13 HCP's. The logic behind this excellent point-of-policy is that the accuracy of Ogust occasionally misfires when describing even a normal range weak two bid, and to be able to handle their broader range the opponents must have unusual agreements. These agreements by their very nature are far too complex to give the opponents a fair shake in a two-board movement.

By now it is apparent that the undisciplined weak two is a losing tactic, but it will still appear at the tournament table. The best approach to defending against it is to compete in customary fashion. However, if you feel the need for a special gadget, an ancient treatment called 'Fishbein' will work most often. Fishbein works as follows. Treat direct doubles as strongly penalty suggestive and use the next higher ranking suit for a takeout bid. While there are problems with this time-honored convention, it is an excellent way to inflict damage on undisciplined opposition. To portray this theme, assume RHO opens with an imaginative two hearts. The following hands define the pluses and minuses of playing Fishbein.

a. ♠AJ5 ♥AQT72 ♦A53 ♣32
b. ♠AT64 ♥J ♦KJ64 ♣AJ42
c. ♠AKT97 ♥J54 ♦AQ98 ♣5

Hand (a) is the reason for playing the convention. This is going to be a disaster for the opponents. Without the use of Fishbein, an awkward bidding situation develops. A takeout double is out of the question, 2NT is a dangerous overbid and partner may not make a balancing double. With hand (b) bid two spades (the equivalent of a takeout double). Responder only has a problem with a sub-minimum hand and spades (e.g. ♠K532 ♥9854 ♦T32 ♣75). In this case, 'pass' works since hand (b) is a minimum takeout. However, if the takeout bidder's hand were better, responder might play a part score when game is cold. Hand (c) is the terror of Fishbein players. Since two spades is conventionally a takeout double, the correct distributional picture is difficult to convey.

As noted above, my feeling is that normalcy is the appropriate winning tactic. Use the standard competitive methods in chapter IV, treating the opposing call as any other weak two bid. Remember, the only people the opponents are hurting are themselves. However, a word of advice: watch for occasions of remarkable bidding judgement. As an example, assume the opponents open two hearts (0-11 HCP's). Everyone passes, the opening lead is made and dummy tables:

♠AQT9 ♥KT ♦AK97 ♣J764

Without a game try, this is an impossible pass. Further, as the play proceeds it turns out that dummy indeed made an excellent decision; opener held a random 4-5 point hand with six mediocre hearts, and eight or nine tricks was the limit of the hand. Since dummy did not make a game try, it should be obvious that, barring telepathy, he knew that opener held sub-minimum values. This comes under the heading of a private understanding and, under current ACBL statutes, is illegal. It's time to call the director.

Another modern subject of interest is the technique of competing against the standard weak two bid. Aside from normal risks, certain distributional hands are close to unbidable. Among these hands are the medium range 5-5 shapes. Assume RHO bids two spades, holding ♠K2 ♥QT984 ♦AKQ75 ♣3 nothing seems attractive. A takeout double, planning to correct partner's predictable three club response to three diamonds, is certainly shape descriptive but grossly exaggerates general strength. A three diamond bid is unnatural, and if the auction becomes competitive, the heart suit may get lost in the shuffle. A three heart call poses a similar problem with regard to losing a spectacular diamond fit. Of course, pass is a bid that won't even be considered.

During the last decade, a method was devised to handle this problem. Against a major suit weak two, a cuebid shows both minors, while a jump to four of a minor would show that minor and the opposite major. Here is this simple yet useful solution in tabular form:

I. Versus a weak two heart opening:
    a. 3H = 5-5 in clubs and diamonds
    b. 4C = 5-5 in clubs and spades
    c. 4D = 5-5 in diamonds and spades
II. Versus a weak two spade opening
    a. 3S = 5-5 in clubs and diamonds
    b. 4C = 5-5 in clubs and hearts
    c. 4D = 5-5 in diamonds and hearts

Presto, all 5-5 problems are solved! The following three hands illustrate this treatment in action.

```
                    ♠ 5
                    ♥ T43
                    ♦ A9854
                    ♣ QJ92
      ♠ KT96                        ♠ Q2
      ♥ A95                         ♥ KQJ872
      ♦ J                           ♦ 62
      ♣ AK653                       ♣ 874
                    ♠ AJ8743
                    ♥ 6
                    ♦ KQT73
                    ♣ T
```

North	East	South	West
	2H	4D	4H
5D	Pass	Pass	Dbl
Pass	Pass	Pass	

This hand from a knockout match illustrates this high-tech defense against the weak two bid. After South's two suited overcall, North had little trouble bidding five diamonds. West's only decision was how to lose the least number of points; two aces and a ruff beat five hearts. Needless to say, "double" turned out to be most expensive since North had little trouble setting up the spade suit for +750. At the other table, N-S were employing more primitive methods and the auction went quietly:

North	East	South	West
	2H	2S	4H
Pass	Pass	Pass	

North's final pass could be described as cowardly by some and prudent by others. The aggressive bidders believe that South must bid five diamonds since North must have a fit for one of the suits. South pointed out that if North held an unsuitable hand like ♠5 ♥T543 ♦82 ♣QJ9652 the vulnerable

134

penalty could be gigantic. Whatever the postmortem result, please notice that the first auction took South off the hook by involving North in the decision making process.

North-South Vulnerable

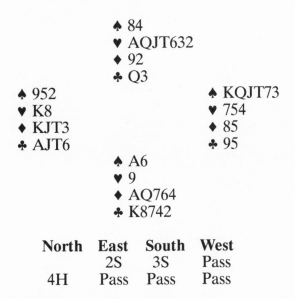

```
                    ♠ 84
                    ♥ AQJT632
                    ♦ 92
                    ♣ Q3
♠ 952                               ♠ KQJT73
♥ K8                                ♥ 754
♦ KJT3                              ♦ 85
♣ AJT6                              ♣ 95
                    ♠ A6
                    ♥ 9
                    ♦ AQ764
                    ♣ K8742
```

North	East	South	West
	2S	3S	Pass
4H	Pass	Pass	Pass

Despite the brevity of this auction, there are some genuine points of interest. After East's opening bid, West planned some sort of supportive action. When RHO indicated both minor suits, he changed his posture. It looked as if North-South were going to walk into some nasty distribution and West readied his axe for the potentially profitable double. When North bid four hearts, creating new complications, South could pass with a clear conscience. The two suited overcall gave him a chance to get the whole hand off his chest with one bid, and he knew that North must have a self sufficient heart suit. West did not have such an easy time of it. The auction changed from a sure profit to a nasty decision. Despite the poor placement of his heart king, his minor suit holdings were excellent defensive values. As it turns out, East-West have a relatively inexpensive sacrifice against the vulnerable North-South game, but fearing the specter of the phantom sacrifice, West made the wrong decision and passed. As with the previous hand, the use of a specialized overcall convention simplified what might have been a very dangerous competitive auction.

East-West Vulnerable

```
                    ♠ 843
                    ♥ Q875
                    ♦ 976
                    ♣ K97
  ♠ T7                          ♠ KQJ962
  ♥ A94                         ♥ 6
  ♦ AKJ542                      ♦ Q83
  ♣ A5                          ♣ 862
                    ♠ A5
                    ♥ KJT32
                    ♦ --
                    ♣ QJT43
```

North	East	South	West
Pass	2S	4C	4S
5H!	Pass	Pass	??

This is another example of being able to describe one's entire hand as a prelude to the winning bid. In the face of partner's two suited overcall, North's push to five hearts was clear-cut and showed both trust and concept. The key is that South claimed to have a great deal of useful distribution. On that basis, he promoted both his four card heart holding and his club king. West was in a lot of trouble; as the cards lie, five hearts doubled will cost a mere 100 points, while five spades goes down with a diamond ruff.

Another competitive problem comes from the fourth hand perspective on hands ranging from terrible to medium to mediocre. This auction presents special difficulties for the competing pair:

North	East	South	West
		Pass	2S
Dbl	Pass	??	

With ♠A4 ♥KT542 ♦432 ♣432 South bids three hearts, but he also would bid three hearts holding ♠J4 ♥T9542 ♦432 ♣432. The takeout doubler, holding ♠98 ♥AQJ5 ♦AQ2 ♣KQ96, now has a totally blind decision. With eighteen HCP's and a good trump fit it is very tempting to press on. Is it correct to bid game or is pass the politic action? Opposite a hand like the second one, the three level is more than high enough. Opposite the first hand, however, four hearts is a good proposition.

Similarly, with ♠K3 ♥AT98 ♦A3 ♣AKQ53 in the same auction as above a decision must be made when partner bids three diamonds. If partner is nice enough to hold ♠764 ♥J7 ♦KQT964 ♣76, 3NT (even 6 diamonds, with careful play) is a fine contract. But if partner holds ♠764 ♥32 ♦J87642 ♣76 there are few tricks forthcoming in anything but a diamond part score.

Clearly, this dilemma can only be resolved if responder has a way to let the doubler know if his hand is at all useful. To deal with this, many partnerships agree that a 2NT response to a takeout double is Lebensohl, requesting that the takeout doubler bid 3 clubs to allow responder to describe a very weak hand. Thus, after partner makes a take-out double of a weak two, it is possible to distinguish between a mediocre hand and a terrible hand. Holding absolute junk (♠32 ♥J9853 ♦Q874 ♣54), bid 2NT and then 3H over 3C. But holding a slightly better hand (♠32 ♥KJ983 ♦QT95 ♣54) bid 3H. In the first case, partner is warned that the hand holds nothing useful. The second case, although not a particularly good hand, at least has some constructive values if partner does carry on to game. The following hands to help clarify this simple but effective treatment.

```
                  ♠ J92
                  ♥ 83
                  ♦ 94
                  ♣ J97543
  ♠ 95                          ♠ KQT743
  ♥ AJ92                        ♥ 754
  ♦ QT65                        ♦ J3
  ♣ KT6                         ♣ A2
                  ♠ A6
                  ♥ KQT6
                  ♦ AK872
                  ♣ Q8
```

North	East	South	West
Pass	2S	Dbl	Pass
2NT	Pass	3C	Pass
Pass	Pass		

North's 2NT response was Lebensohl in action. South bid 3C as requested which was gratefully passed by North. Hoping to cut down ruffs in the short hand, West led a small club. East won the ace and returned a club to partner's king. West switched to a spade. South ducked, winning the spade continuation. Hoping for the best, he led A-K of diamonds and ruffed a diamond in dummy. When the suit failed to split he led a heart towards his K-Q. West now fell from grace by thoughtlessly capturing the king with the ace. With nothing but red cards, he was well and truly endplayed. A heart lead would be into the Q-T while a diamond would establish the necessary pitch for dummy's losing spade. The important thing is that due to Lebensohl, N-S had no trouble reaching their optimum contract.

```
                    ♠ AJT82
                    ♥ T65
                    ♦ 865
                    ♣ K9
    ♠ 7643                          ♠ 9
    ♥ 872                           ♥ KQJ943
    ♦ J3                            ♦ T94
    ♣ AT65                          ♣ Q84
                    ♠ KQ5
                    ♥ A
                    ♦ AKQ72
                    ♣ J732
```

North	East	South	West
Pass	2H	Dbl	Pass
2NT	Pass	3C	Pass
3S	Pass	4H	Pass
5C	Pass	6S	Pass
Pass	Pass		

This auction illustrates another aspect of Lebensohl. With a poor hand, North could have bid a simple two spades. With this knowledge, the use of Lebensohl followed by three spades is invitational, asking partner to bid game with extra values. Of course, South had no problem accepting the invitation, but was there more? With inadequate information, South indicated his slam interest by cue bidding four hearts (with a monster hand and hearts he would have bid 3♥ over 2NT). North decided that in the face of the bidding he held a good hand; his trump suit was of good quality and the club king rated to be a useful card. As a result, he found the master bid of five clubs, revealing his only side honor card. This was enough for South to leap directly to the small slam in spades.

Lebensohl is a useful, risk-free technique for defining the quality of responder's three level bid to a takeout double. To those familiar with Lebensohl in competitive NT auctions, it is already terra cognita. If unfamiliar, it is relatively simple to learn and well worth the effort.

In the first part of this chapter, we considered a style best described as 'sharp practice' while in the second we dealt with simple though effective high tech competitive methods.

As we all know, bidding is a language with limited vocabulary, and as a result theoreticians constantly search for new and more efficient ways to describe their hands. Occasionally, this search produces a useful descriptive innovation like the weak two bid. Occasionally, however, the search turns up a method where the complications may outweigh the added accuracy. One example of this is the Multi-Colored Two Diamond opening bid.

Of British origin, the Multi-Colored Two Diamond opening, known affectionately as "Multi" to its devotees, is a brilliant though highly convoluted convention showing either a major suit weak two bid, a three suited hand containing 17-24 HCP's, or a balanced 21-22 HCP's. The following schedule of responses and rebids should illustrate why despite its advantages, multi is not for the casual once a week club player.

I. 2D opening = one of the following hand types
    A. a weak two heart opening
    B. a weak two spade opening
    C. 4-4-4-1 (any singleton) 17-24 HCP's
    D. 21-22 HCP's no trump shape

II. Responders Options
    A. 2H = Two-level signoff in partner's weak two bid suit.
       1. Opener passes with a weak two in hearts
       2. Opener bids two spades with a weak two in spades
       3. Opener bids 2NT with 21-22 no trump shape
       4. Opener bids at the 3-level with 4-4-4-1
          a. 3C = 4-4-1-4 (singleton diamond)
          b. 3D = 4-1-4-4 (singleton heart)
          c. 3H = 1-4-4-4 (singleton spade)
          d. 3S = 4-4-4-1 (singleton club)

B. 2S = a two way bid showing either a signoff opposite weak two spade opening or invitational values opposite a weak two heart opening.
   1. Opener passes with a weak two in spades
   2. Opener bids 2N with 21-22 HCP's (no trump shape)
   3. Opener clarifies with a weak two in hearts
      a. 3C = good weak two bid
      b. 3H = poor weak two bid
      c. Other suit bids = various 4-4-4-1s

C. 2N = forcing and asking

D. 3N = 4H + 4S; preemptive opposite a weak two bid

III. Openers' Rebids (after 2D - 2NT)
   A. Three-level suit bids = weak two bids
      1. 3C = maximum (hearts); 3D asks trump quality
         a. 3H = poor trumps
         b. 3S = good trumps
      2. 3D = maximum (spades); 3H asks trump quality
         a. 3S = poor trumps
         b. 3N = good trumps
      3. 3H = minimum (hearts)
      4. 3S = minimum (spade)

   B. 3NT = 21-22 HCP's (notrump shape)

   C. Four-level bids = three 4 card suits, 17-24 HCP's
      1. 4C = 4-4-1-4 (singleton diamond)
      2. 4D = 4-1-4-4 (singleton heart)
      3. 4H = 1-4-4-4 (singleton spade)
      4. 4S = 4-4-4-1 (singleton club)

There's more! All of the strong no trump sequences employ standard methods including Stayman, Jacoby, et al. All of the 4-4-4-1 sequences have added wrinkles based on responder bidding openers' singleton. Such things as narrowing the point range, specifying control cards (aces and kings) and even Blackwood for queens. All this is very nice, but to quote the Duke of Wellington when watching a bunch of green recruits on drill, "I have no idea how the enemy will react to their antics but by God they frighten me!"

Well, the Multi shouldn't be frightening. There are several methods to equalize its effect on the auction. The simplest is a transfer takeout sequence. Thus a direct seat double is the same as a takeout double of 2H, and a direct bid of 2H is a takeout double of 2S. The entire structure follows:

    I.   Double = Takeout of Hearts
    II.   2H = Takeout of Spades
    III. 2S = Both minors, like the unusual NT.
    IV. 2NT = a standard NT overcall
    V.   3 Minor = invitational to 3NT

After 2♦ - Pass - 2♥(♠) - ?, roughly the same scheme applies. Now, double is a takeout bid of the other major. I will leave further ramifications of this structure to the reader, knowing that the exposure to Multi Two Diamonds will be limited.

Has bridge really come to this? Aside from the complexities, the ACBL currently prohibits Multi in all but multiple session nationally rated events (Super chart). If this is the case, why is it included in this book? First, it is healthy to know about it without having to resort to constant alerts (in a method as complex as this, the opponents are just as likely to be alerting each other). Secondly, your partnership may desire to learn this convention for purposes of top level competition, and it's difficult to find a schedule of Multi Two Diamond bids and responses. Now there is one at the tail end of *Weak Two Bid in Bridge*!

Bon Chance!

Harold Feldheim has been a gamesman from an early age. Not only is he an expert at bridge, he is also proficient at Chess, Go and Backgammon. His previous texts, *Swiss Team Tactics* and *Five Card Majors* have become standard teaching references. He produced the first computerized teacher, "Charles Goren Teaches Bridge," which won the *BYTE* education award in 1984.

He is an active bridge teacher, both at the table and in the classroom. Often found at a bridge tournament, watching his students become masters in their own right is his greatest pleasure.

Harold lives in Hamden, Connecticut with his wife, Susan, and his dog, Cassiopeia.

Also from C & T Bridge Supplies:

Harold Feldheim

Doubles in Competition (spring 92)   5.95

> *Negative and Responsive Doubles* expanded and updated for the 90's. Now includes competitive, support and action doubles.

Bridge Tactics (spring 92)   12.95

> Destined to be a classic, this book discusses expert bidding situations. In it you will learn when to bid holding no cards and when to pass when holding the deck.

Larry Harris

Bridge Player's Companion   11.95

> Presents a clear and concise synopsis of the rules of the game as well as some basic tactical information. Invaluable for the up and coming player.

Michael Lawrence

The Lebensohl Convention   1.95
Jacoby & Texas Transfers   1.95
Major Suit Raises   4.95

Marshall Miles

All 52 Cards (spring 92)   9.95

> At last this long time classic has been reprinted. Now completely updated to reflect both the changing bidding styles and the newest play and carding agreements.

For these or any other books or equipment related to the game of bridge please give us a call.

1 (800) 525-4718